Zen and the Art of Doing F*ckng Nothing (and Doing It Well)

31 Paths to Outrageously Epic, Chill-Like-You-DGAF Paradise

S. Madeira

Copyright © 2025 by S. Madeira

All rights reserved. No part of this publication may be reproduced, distributed, stored in a retrieval system, or transmitted in any form or by any means—electronic, mechanical, photocopying, recording, scanning, or otherwise—without the prior written permission of the author or publisher, except in the case of brief quotations embodied in critical reviews, academic works, or articles, provided full attribution is given.

First Edition: 2025

Cover design by didiwahyudi.trend

This publication is intended for informational, educational, and entertainment purposes only. It does not constitute professional medical, psychological, therapeutic, or legal advice. The author and publisher make no representations or warranties concerning the accuracy or applicability of the content contained in this book.

Neither the author nor the publisher shall be held liable for any loss, damage, or injury allegedly arising from any information or suggestion in this book.

All characters, stories, and personal experiences described herein are either the product of the author's imagination, used with permission, or adapted to protect confidentiality. Any resemblance to actual persons, living or dead, is purely coincidental unless otherwise stated.

Table of Contents

Introduction Welcome to Absolutely Nothing (You're Already Doing Great)	1
Zen One The Sacred Art of Staring at the Ceiling	4
Zen Two How to Nap Like a Spiritual Warrior	8
Zen Three Breathing; You're Already Doing It, Chill	12
Zen Four Why Your Couch Is Actually a Meditation Cushion in Disguise	17
Zen Five Time Isn't Real and Neither Is Your To-Do List	22
Zen Six Existential Dread, But Make It Cozy	27
Zen Seven Becoming One with the Carpet	32

Zen Eight Daydreaming as a Divine Right	37
Zen Nine The Universe Doesn't Care If You Fold the Laundry	42
Zen Ten Overthinking Is Just Advanced Sitting	47
Zen Eleven Scrolling with Awareness (and Low Expectations)	52
Zen Twelve Zen and the Art of Saying "Nope"	56
Zen Thirteen Ghosting Guilt Like a Ninja Monk	61
Zen Fourteen Procrastination as a Portal to the Divine	66
Zen Fifteen Meditative Snacking and the Sacred Crinkle of the Chip Bag	70
Zen Sixteen How to Politely Decline Every Invitation Forever (Without Losing Friends or Your Soul)	74
Zen Seventeen "Sorry, I Was Meditating", And Other Holy Lies That Work Every Damn Time	80
Zen Eighteen Mindful Ignoring for Beginners (And the Spiritually Advanced)	85

Zen Nineteen Group Naps as a Form of Activism (Viva la REM!)	89
Zen Twenty Dating While Spiritually Unavailable (Swipe Left on Emotional Labor)	94
Zen Twenty-One You Are Enough, Even If You Did Nothing Today	99
Zen Twenty-Two The Tao of Takeout	104
Zen Twenty-Three Letting Go of Ambition Without Crying (Much)	110
Zen Twenty-Four Enlightenment Is Probably Just Low Blood Sugar	113
Zen Twenty-Five When in Doubt, Become One with the Blanket	117
Zen Twenty-Six Canceling Plans as a Form of Self-Care	122
Zen Twenty-Seven The Gentle Art of Not Giving a Sh*t	128
Zen Twenty-Eight Be the Cloud. Float. Judge Nothing. Rain Occasionally.	134
Zen Twenty-Nine Sit. Breathe. Sip. Repeat.	140
Zen Thirty How to Procrastinate with Presence	146
Zen Thirty-One Spiritual Bloating and Other Mystical Conditions	152

Conclusion 157

Appendix A 158
Frequently Unasked Questions (FUQs)

Introduction

WELCOME TO ABSOLUTELY NOTHING (YOU'RE ALREADY DOING GREAT)

Let's get something straight right from the start: this book is not here to help you *achieve more*. It will not teach you to 10x your productivity, find your life's purpose, optimize your routines, or "unlock your best self" by 5 a.m. every morning. If that's what you're after, kindly yeet this book into the sun and back away slowly.

Still here? Excellent. You're exactly who this book is for.

Welcome to the art of doing absolutely f*cking nothing and not just surviving it but thriving in it. This is the ancient (and extremely underrated) spiritual practice of *stopping, sitting, staring at walls,* and *not giving a single glittering damn* about being busy, useful, or impressive. It's Zen, but with crumbs on your shirt and Netflix asking if you're still watching.

Let me guess, you've been over-functioning for most of your adult life. You've been scheduling your leisure time like it's a hostage negotiation, answering emails at red lights, and telling people you're "so busy" with the same pride people used to reserve for *winning a war*. The to-do list is your religion, your calendar looks like a game of Tetris, and rest? Rest is for the weak. Or the dead.

But maybe, just maybe, you're tired. Like, soul-deep tired. Like, the idea of doing "one more thing" makes you want to crawl into a pile of laundry and wait for the world to reset.

Good. You're ready.

This book is a friendly rebellion. A middle finger to hustle culture. A wink to the monk who sat under a tree for 49 days and said, "Nah, I'm good here." It's not about being lazy; although if laziness is your truth, I fully support it. It's about *not performing*. Not striving. Not measuring your worth in checkboxes and burned-out cortisol levels.

In these pages, you'll find the lost wisdom of the nap. The subtle power of staring at the ceiling. The enlightened act of canceling plans because pants are hard. You'll learn that doing nothing isn't a failure; it's a radical, sacred art form. And the best part? You already know how to do it. You've just forgotten. Or been shamed out of it.

We'll explore great spiritual truths like:

- How to achieve Nirvana by lying down and refusing to answer the door.

- Why overthinking is just cardio for the anxious.

- The Zen of scrolling aimlessly and forgetting why you picked up your phone in the first place.

- The mystical power of The Shrug.

You don't need incense. You don't need a guru. You just need to stop giving so many f*cks and let your soul stretch out on the couch for a minute.

So let's begin. Or don't. You can put this book down and take a nap instead. That would be incredibly on-brand.

Either way, welcome to the sacred art of doing nothing.

We've been waiting for you.

And by "we," I mean no one. Because everyone else is out trying too hard.

Namaste, b*tches.

Zen One

THE SACRED ART OF STARING AT THE CEILING

A 10,000-Year-Old Tradition Practiced in Crappy Apartments Worldwide

There's a hallowed, ancient practice that's been handed down through the ages, not by wise sages or sacred texts, but by sheer human laziness and a universal hatred of to-do lists. It requires no fancy yoga pants, no overpriced retreat in the Himalayas, and no guru with a man bun and a superiority complex. All you need is a ceiling, preferably one with a questionable stain you've named "Greg, and a soft surface to flop onto like a spiritually exhausted starfish. Welcome, dear reader, to the sacred art of staring at the ceiling, the ultimate act of doing f*ckng nothing and doing it with flair.

This isn't some casual glance upward while you pretend to care about your smoke detector's battery. Oh no. This is a full-body, spine-to-couch surrender, a horizontal middle finger to the cult of productivity that's been screaming "hustle harder" since you were old enough to have an email inbox. You collapse onto your chosen surface; couch, bed, or that one yoga mat you bought in a fit of optimism and now use as a snack crumb collector. Your eyes drift to the glorious expanse above: cracked, possibly water-damaged, home to a cobweb that's been there so long you've named the spider "Tenant of the Year." That eight-legged freeloader earned its spot, just like you earned this moment of glorious, guilt-free inertia.

The Zen of Upward Apathy

In this meditative state of upward apathy, your brain becomes a cosmic lazy river, thoughts bobbing along like half-inflated pool floaties. "Should I be doing something right now?" Nope, this is it, champ, this is the main event. "Am I wasting time?" Maybe, but wasting time is just capitalism's way of shaming you for not monetizing your every breath. Consider this: how many world-changing ideas, existential meltdowns, or sudden urges to Google "what's that smell in my fridge" started with someone sprawled out, staring at a ceiling, and muttering, "Hmm"? The ceiling has seen it all. Your dreams, your doubts, that one time you tried to "manifest" a pizza delivery without leaving the couch and it's never once judged you. That's more than you can say for your mom's group chat.

This is your moment, free from the tyranny of apps, goals, or that fitness influencer yelling about "pelvic tilts to activate your core." Just you, the ceiling, and the profound realization that you don't have to do a damn thing right now. This isn't laziness; it's a trance of non-doing, a philosophical pause so deep it could make a TED Talk speaker rethink their life. You're not stuck; you're marinating in existential marinade, baby. Enlightenment without the incense, transcendence without the $200 yoga retreat. You're basically Buddha, but with better Wi-Fi and a lingering suspicion that Greg the Ceiling Stain is judging your life choices.

A Portal to Pure, Unfiltered Nope

Some call staring at the ceiling a gateway to dissociation. We call it a portal to Zen, a first-class ticket to the land of Drift, where your mental hard drive defragments and your soul remembers what it's like to not be chased by a Google Calendar notification. It's where you process deep questions, like "Why do I own so many reusable straws?" or "Is my cat plotting against me?" It's where you realize that "productivity" is just a scam to keep you from eating cereal straight from the box while contemplating the meaning of life.

And let's talk about the haters. Some productivity bro in a Patagonia vest will try to shame you, saying, "You're just lying there!" Damn right you are, and you're doing it like a pro. If anyone barges in and asks what you're up to, lock eyes with them, channel the serenity of a monk who's just discovered Netflix, and say, "I'm practicing sacred ceiling contemplation, a 10,000-year-old art form. What are you doing with your life, Chad?" Watch them stammer, back away, and question their entire existence. For extra flair, gesture vaguely at Greg the Stain and whisper, "He's my guru now."

The Ceiling Gazer's Starter Pack

To master this ancient art, you need minimal gear, because effort is the enemy. Here's what you'll need:

- **A Flat Surface:** Couch, bed, or the floor if you're feeling extra rebellious. Bonus points if it's covered in crumbs that spell out "YOLO" in snack residue.

- **A Ceiling:** Any will do, but one with a weird stain or a rogue popcorn texture adds character. Name the imperfections for extra zen points.

- **Optional Snacks**: A bag of chips within arm's reach, because enlightenment is better with a side of salt and vinegar.

- **A Blank Stare**: Practice in the mirror until it says, "I'm not here, but I'm also everywhere." Blink occasionally; eye health matters, even for slackers.

Welcome to the Path of Least Resistance

Staring at the ceiling isn't just a pastime; it's a lifestyle, a sacred rebellion against a world that wants you to "seize the day" when you'd rather seize a nap. It's you, Greg the Stain, and that cobweb spider living your best, most pointless lives together. So go ahead—sprawl out, stare up, and let the universe figure itself out for a while. You're not lazy; you're a ceiling-gazing visionary, a pioneer of non-doing, a goddamn poet of pause.

Blink occasionally. Hydrate if you feel like it. And if anyone tries to drag you back to the grind, just point to the ceiling and say, "Talk to Greg. He's got my schedule." Welcome to the path of less resistance, you horizontal, zen-tastic legend.

Zen Two

How to Nap Like a Spiritual Warrior

Close Your Eyes. Open Your Third One. Snore Like a Cosmic Chainsaw.

Some call it a "nap." We call it advanced consciousness training, a mystical middle finger to a world obsessed with hustle, ambition, and 87 flavors of overpriced oat milk lattes. Napping isn't just for sticky-fingered toddlers or cats who side-eye you from their 17th snooze of the day. It's for spiritual warriors: badass, blanket-wielding rebels who know the bravest thing you can do in a society that worships "grind" is to say, "Screw it," and flop face-first into a pile of pillows like a divinely exhausted walrus.

But don't get it twisted: a spiritual warrior doesn't just collapse onto the nearest surface like a retired sea lion with a Netflix subscription. Oh no, this is a sacred ritual, a choreographed descent into the holy land of Do-Nothing-Nirvana. You choose your battlefield with care: the couch (crumb-dusted, loyal), the bed (unmade, judgmental), or that one sunbeam on the floor that's basically begging you to curl up in it like a spiritually enlightened housecat. You gather your armor: a weighted blanket so heavy it could anchor a ship, a fortress of pillows (minimum five, because one is for amateurs), and a sleepy-time tea you'll absolutely forget to drink because you're already halfway to Snoozeville.

The Ritual of Radical Repose

Before you dive into the abyss of REM, you set the stage. Silence your phone, not out of discipline, but because your thumb is too zen to bother with the "Do Not Disturb" button. Dim the lights, or don't, because who has the energy to get up? If you're feeling extra, light a candle that smells like "forest vibes" or "inner peace and petty grudges." Then, the descent begins. You sink into your chosen surface, your body melting like a popsicle in a microwave. Your breathing slows to a rhythm that says, "I'm one exhale away from becoming a cloud."

Thoughts will try to crash the party: "Should I check my email?" Hell no. "Did I lock the door?" Probably not, but thieves can't steal your vibe. "Is this what failure feels like?" Absolutely not, Karen, this is what surrender feels like, and it's glorious. You're not just napping; you're dropping out of your overcaffeinated brain and into your parasympathetic power, regulating your nervous system like a cosmic IT guy rebooting a crashed server. You're recharging, restoring, and, let's be real, snoring so loud you could wake a coma patient in the next zip code. That's not laziness; that's horizontal healing incarnate, a one-person protest against the cult of "rise and grind" that's been gaslighting you since you got your first day planner.

The Sacred Side Effects

There's no shame in waking up from a nap looking like you just survived a time warp. You're sweaty, disoriented, with pillow creases on your face that could pass for ancient runes. Your mouth tastes like regret and last night's tacos, and you're not entirely sure if it's 3 p.m. or the year 2047. That's not failure;

that's proof you went deep, warrior. Maybe you visited a dream realm where you were a mermaid running a taco truck. Maybe you communed with your past lives, one of which was definitely a sloth with excellent boundaries. Or maybe you just drooled so much you've created a new ecosystem on your couch cushion. It's all sacred, okay? You're not gross; you're a moist mystic.

And let's talk about the haters. Some productivity bro with a smartwatch and a protein shake will try to shame you: "You're sleeping in the middle of the day?" Damn right you are, and you're doing it like a pro. If someone knocks on your door mid-nap, don't panic. Channel the serenity of a monk who's just discovered edibles, rise (slowly, because vertigo is real), and whisper through the crack, "I was meditating... aggressively. Come back when you've unlocked your third eye." Then slam the door, flop back down, and resume your holy snooze. The world can wait; your REM cycle cannot.

The Spiritual Warrior's Nap Kit

To nap like a true badass, you need the right gear. Keep it minimal, because effort is the enemy:

- **A Nap Throne**: Couch, bed, or that one rug you bought at IKEA because it "felt like your soul's texture." Crumbs are optional but encouraged.

- **A Weighted Blanket**: Minimum 20 pounds, because you're not just napping; you're being hugged by the universe (or at least by gravity).

- **A Pillow Fortress**: Stack 'em high. One for your head, one for your knees, one to hug like it's your emotional support animal, and two for vibes.

- **A Snack Stash**: Stash some Goldfish crackers nearby, because spiritual warriors need fuel, and chewing is basically cardio.

- **A Fan or White Noise Machine**: Set it to "gentle breeze" or "distant thunderstorm" to drown out the sound of your neighbor's leaf blower or your own existential dread.

Napping Is Resistance

Napping isn't just self-care; it's activism, a radical rejection of a society that thinks "busy" is a personality trait. Every snooze is a protest against the 5 a.m. hustle, the 9-to-5 grind, and the expectation that you should answer emails when you're still processing last night's dream about a sentient burrito. You're not lazy; you're a monk-sloth hybrid, a pioneer of pause, a goddamn poet of the pillow. You're restoring the balance of the cosmos, one drool-soaked nap at a time.

So go ahead, brave napper. Ignore the productivity cult. Embrace your inner couch potato guru. When the world tries to drag you back to its chaos, just roll over, pull that blanket tighter, and mutter, "I'm on a spiritual quest, and my quest is to stay horizontal." Close your eyes, open your third one, and nap like the radiant, rebellious warrior you are. The revolution can wait; you've got zzz's to catch.

Zen Three

Breathing; You're Already Doing It, Chill

An Enlightenment Guide for Anyone with Functional Lungs

Let's talk about breathing, that thing you're doing right now without a shred of effort, like a multitasking legend who's also scrolling through cat memes and ignoring a sink full of dishes. You've been inhaling and exhaling since you slid out of the womb, yet somehow, the modern self-help industrial complex has decided you're screwing it up. Apparently, you need a $299 online course, a smartwatch that nags you to "breathe mindfully," and a Himalayan monk named Kevin with a man bun and a suspiciously perfect Spotify playlist to teach you how to not die. Spoiler alert: you're already a breathing pro, and Kevin can keep his lavender-scented TED Talk.

Breathing has become a freaking Olympic sport, complete with jargon that sounds like it was invented by a yoga influencer mid-kale smoothie. "Box breathing." "Lion's breath." "Two inhales, one exhale, hum like a bumblebee while visualizing a purple goat doing downward dog." There are apps that rate your breath like it's applying for a mortgage, and retreats where people pay to sit in a circle and hyperventilate competitively. But here's the dirty little secret your favorite wellness guru won't whisper over their $18 green juice: you're already breathing. Congrats, champ; you're a natural-born lung legend, and you didn't even need to chant "om" to get there.

The Radical Act of Not Overthinking It

This chapter isn't about "fixing" your breath or turning your lungs into overachieving productivity machines. It's about realizing your breath is already out here doing the Lord's work, keeping you alive without a single Post-it note or motivational poster. You don't need to "biohack" your exhale or "optimize" your inhale like you're tweaking a spreadsheet for your boss. You just need to notice, every once in a while, that your body is pulling off something miraculous, boring, and downright sexy every second: keeping you from keeling over without your micromanaging ass getting in the way.

Here's a wild idea: try doing nothing. Sit down (or lie down, or drape yourself over the couch like an existentially exhausted octopus who's just quit its day job). Instead of "taking" a breath like you're shoplifting oxygen from a Goop pop-up store, let it roll in like a lazy cloud on a Netflix binge. Feel it drift through your nostrils, all chill and unbothered. Then let it leave like your last shred of motivation on a Monday morning, floating away without a care. Don't force it. Don't count it like some Type-A weirdo timing their inhales to a metronome. Don't judge it like it's auditioning for American Idol. Just exist with it. That's called presence, baby, and you didn't even need to light a $45 sage bundle to get there.

The Wellness Industrial Complex Hates This One Trick

Sure, "intentional" breathing has benefits. It can calm your frazzled nervous system, lower your blood pressure, and maybe stop you from yeeting a folding chair at the IKEA checkout line when they're out of meatballs. But the real magic isn't in the technique; it's in the permission. Permission to stop. To feel. To do absolutely jack squat. In a world that wants you to hustle, grind, and "lean in" until you're leaning into a nervous breakdown, the most radical thing you can do is plop onto your couch, breathe like a chill sea cucumber, and tell productivity culture to go shove its vision board where the sun don't shine.

Think about it: your lungs are out here putting in overtime, no PTO, no complaints, while you're busy stressing over whether you "liked" your coworker's LinkedIn post fast enough. They're the unsung heroes of your body, working 24/7 so you can waste hours Googling "Why does my cat stare at walls?" or arguing with your Roomba because it got stuck under the couch again. Your breath doesn't need a performance review; it needs a high-five and maybe a snack break.

The Anti-Breathing Bootcamp

If you must practice breathing (because apparently existing isn't enough), here's the laziest, most zen approach possible:

- **Find a Spot**: Couch, bed, or that one corner of the floor where the Wi-Fi signal is strongest. Bonus points if there's a snack crumb constellation spelling out "YOLO."

- **Get Comfy**: Slouch, sprawl, or contort yourself into a position that would make a chiropractor weep. Comfort is king.

- **Breathe, Duh**: Notice your breath like it's a friend who showed up unannounced with pizza. Don't control it; just vibe with it.

- **Ignore the Noise**: If thoughts like "Did I pay my electric bill?" or "Is my neighbor's dog plotting against me?" creep in, let them float away like a bad Tinder match.

- **Optional Flair**: Hum softly if you feel fancy, but only if it's less effort than scrolling through TikTok.

No apps. No timers. No purple goats. Just you, your lungs, and the sweet, sweet freedom of not giving a crap about "diaphragmatic optimization."

Handling the Breathing Police

The next time some wellness bro in a $200 athleisure set tells you to "breathe deeper" or "try 4-7-8 breathing," just smile, nod, and hit them with, "Thanks, but I've been crushing this breathing game since birth. How's your lung game, Chad?" If your yoga teacher starts ranting about "pranayama for peak performance," channel the serenity of a sloth on a spa day and say, "I'm practicing the ancient art of Not Overthinking My Oxygen Intake. It's very exclusive." Then flop onto your mat and fake a nap for extra zen points.

And if anyone—your mom, your boss, that one friend who's always "just checking in"—says, "Don't forget to breathe," give them a slow, dramatic blink and reply, "Don't worry, I've got 30 years of uninterrupted lung experience. I'm basically a breathing influencer now." Then walk away, ideally with a scarf trailing behind you for maximum mystical effect.

Breathe Like Nobody's Judging

Breathing isn't just survival; it's rebellion. It's your body saying, "I got you, fam," while the world screams at you to hustle harder, multitask better, and "seize the day" when you'd rather seize a bag of chips. So keep breathing, you lung-wielding legend. Keep vibing with your inhales and exhales like they're your oldest friends who never ask for Venmo repayments. You're not just alive; you're a chill sea cucumber in a sea of overachievers, and that's the most enlightened thing you can be.

So go ahead, sprawl out, breathe like it's no big deal (because it isn't), and let the universe figure out its own drama. You've got oxygen, a couch, and zero reasons to care about Kevin's breathing workshop. Namaste, you effortless, air-sucking icon.

Zen Four

WHY YOUR COUCH IS ACTUALLY A MEDITATION CUSHION IN DISGUISE

A Revelation in Crumb-Covered Upholstery and Zero-Effort Enlightenment

Listen up, because we're about to blow the lid off the meditation industrial complex: you don't need a $200 handwoven zafu blessed by Himalayan monks who've never heard of Wi-Fi to achieve nirvana. You don't need a yoga studio that smells like patchouli and performative serenity. You've already got the ultimate spiritual sanctuary, and it's been sitting in your living room, collecting potato chip crumbs and questionable stains since you impulse-bought it during a Black Friday sale. That's right, your couch, that glorious, Netflix-soaked, sweatpants-stained throne of modern sloth, is a meditation cushion in disguise. You're not lazy; you're a couch-bound Buddha, and your upholstery is your ticket to enlightenment.

Forget those wellness influencers with their "you must sit upright, legs folded, spine straighter than a corporate ladder" nonsense. That's adorable, but real meditation? It happens when your butt has fused with a cushion that knows your curves better than your best friend knows your coffee order. It happens in sweatpants so worn they're practically a second skin. It happens with a half-eaten bag of Goldfish within arm's reach and a vague plan to "maybe vacuum later" that you both know is a lie. Your couch doesn't care if your third eye is crusted shut from last night's existential crisis or if your chakras are tangled like dollar-store earbuds in a junk drawer. It just holds you, cradling your chaos like the Buddha would if he were microfiber, slightly reclined, and had a built-in cupholder.

The Couch as Cosmic Guru

Let's talk about why your couch is the unsung hero of your spiritual journey. Traditionalists might drone on about lotus pose and "aligning your spine to the cosmos," but your couch laughs in the face of such high-effort dogma. It's literally engineered for stillness, designed to seduce you into doing less with every plush, crumb-dusted inch. Slouch? Sacred. Sprawled sideways like a toppled Greek statue? Divine. One leg dangling off the armrest while the other's lost in a blanket burrito? That's peak enlightenment, baby. The only thing you need to align is your vibe, and your couch is the ultimate vibe curator, whispering, "Stay here, you majestic disaster. The world can wait."

Your couch doesn't judge. It's seen you cry during a Great British Bake Off finale, rage-scroll through your ex's Instagram, and "accidentally" eat an entire family-sized bag of Cheetos in one sitting. It's held you through existential meltdowns, hungover Sundays, and that one time you tried to "manifest" a pizza delivery without leaving the cushions. And yet, it never once asked you to "activate your core" or "visualize your highest self." It's the most enlightened thing in your apartment, and that includes your overpriced Himalayan salt lamp named Gerald.

The Lazy Zen Meditation Protocol

The next time you think, "I should meditate, but I'm already on the couch," congratulations; you're halfway to nirvana. You don't need to haul your ass to a meditation retreat or sit cross-legged until your knees stage a coup. You're already in the perfect position, literally and metaphysically. Here's how to turn your couch session into a full-blown spiritual flex:

- **Settle In**: Sink into your couch like it's a hug from the universe. Ignore the stray popcorn kernel poking your thigh; it's just testing your resolve.

- **Breathe, or Whatever**: Take a lazy breath, or don't. Your lungs are already clocking in for the shift, so no need to micromanage.

- **Add Optional Flair**: Light a candle if you're feeling extra (or just flick on Gerald the Salt Lamp for ambiance). Hold a crystal, a lukewarm coffee mug, or that one remote you haven't found the batteries for; it's all holy if you're present.

- **Let Thoughts Drift**: If your brain starts yammering about unpaid bills or whether your cat is secretly a government spy, let it ramble. Your couch is a judgment-free zone.

- **Nap If You Want**: If you drift off, that's not failure; that's advanced consciousness training. Drool is just your soul's glitter.

Boom. You're meditating. No apps, no gurus, no $300 "sound bath" required. Your couch is your zafu, your ashram, your whole damn vibe temple.

The Couch Gazer's Starter Pack

To maximize your couch's spiritual potential, you need minimal gear—because effort is the enemy of enlightenment:

- **A Crumb-Dusted Couch**: Bonus points if it's got a stain you've named (shoutout to Greg, the mystery splotch from that one wild Taco Tuesday).

- **A Throw Blanket**: Your robe of enlightenment, preferably one that smells like "cozy" and "I haven't done laundry in two weeks."

- **A Remote**: Your bell of mindfulness. Clicking through channels counts as a mantra, especially if you land on Pawn Stars reruns.

- **Snacks**: A bag of chips or a rogue granola bar wedged between the cushions. Enlightenment tastes better with salt.

- **A Vibe**: That's it. Just show up as your messy, slouchy self. Your couch is ready to meet you where you're at.

Handling the Meditation Snobs

When some yoga bro in a $150 tank top tells you meditation requires a "proper cushion" and a "sacred space," laugh so hard you spill your coffee. Then hit them with, "My couch is my zafu, my ashram, and my therapist, all in one glorious, stain-covered package. What's your furniture doing for your soul, Brad?" If your mom calls and asks why you're "wasting the day" on the couch, channel the serenity of a sloth on a spa day and say, "I'm communing with the divine microfiber, Mom. It's a whole spiritual thing." Then mute her and go back to your Pawn Stars marathon.

Your couch is more than furniture; it's a movement. It's a rebellion against a world that demands you "lean in" when you'd rather lean back. It's a reminder that you don't need to twist yourself into a pretzel or chant in Sanskrit to find peace. You just need to sink in, stay put, and let your couch work its magic. So sit, slouch, maybe nap. You're not just chilling; you're meditating like a goddamn upholstery guru. Welcome to the path of least resistance, you crumb-dusted, couch-hugging legend.

Zen Five

Time Isn't Real and Neither Is Your To-Do List

An Existential Crisis in Glittery Bullet Points

Buckle up, because we're about to yeet the concept of time into the cosmic void where it belongs. Time? It's a scam, cooked up by stressed-out weirdos in ancient Mesopotamia who needed an excuse to be late for chariot carpools. Clocks? Bald-faced lies with hands that mock your existence. Calendars? Just overpriced paper traps designed to guilt you into "scheduling joy." And that "urgent" need to clear your inbox before lunch? Pure capitalist fan fiction, written by someone who's never known the bliss of eating cereal at 3 p.m. in their underwear.

Here's the tea: in the infinite, vibey NOW of the universe, your to-do list is about as meaningful as a crumpled Starbucks receipt from 2017 or that one email from your boss titled "Q3 Synergy Goals." It's just noise, dressed up in color-coded Post-its and Google Calendar notifications that scream, "You're a failure unless you check me off by EOD!" But lean in, because here's the mind-blowing truth: when you stop worshipping time like it's a vengeful deity, something magical happens, guilt evaporates. That sneaky gremlin that creeps in when you're binge-watching

Nailed It! instead of "optimizing your workflow"? Gone. Poof. When you realize time isn't real, you also realize you're not "behind." You're not procrastinating. You're just being, you radiant, cereal-slurping star. Wild, right?

Your To-Do List Is Just Bad Fanfic

Let's talk about that to-do list, looming over you like a judgmental aunt at a family reunion. Newsflash: it's not a sacred contract etched in cosmic stone. It's a bunch of half-baked suggestions scribbled by your past self, who was probably hopped up on three espressos and wildly overestimated your future self's enthusiasm for "organizing the spice rack." You're allowed to look at it, laugh like a villain in a B-movie, and say, "Nah, Past Me, you were trippin'." That list doesn't own you; it's basically just a Pinterest board for your anxiety.

Monks spend lifetimes sitting under trees, watching leaves fall, and calling it enlightenment. You spent four hours watching a cooking show you'll never cook from, Googling "can you air-fry a whole pizza," and accidentally napping through a Zoom meeting. Same energy, different aesthetic. Presence is presence, whether you're contemplating the universe or contemplating whether your cat's side-eye means he's plotting your demise. You're not slacking; you're a non-doing visionary, a pioneer of pause, a goddamn poet of procrastination.

How to Dismantle the Time Tyranny

Ready to kick time and its to-do list minions to the curb? Here's your lazy-zen guide to existential rebellion:

- **Toss the Planner**: Chuck it in a drawer, or better yet, repurpose it as a sketchbook for your masterpiece doodles of cats wearing berets. Enlightenment looks better with whiskers.

- **Rename Your Tasks**: Turn "laundry" into "sacred folding ceremony to honor the divine chaos of socks." Rewrite "reply to emails" as "embrace digital impermanence by letting Gmail crash my soul." Suddenly, your list is a spiritual vision board, not a guillotine.

- **Ritualize the Rejection**: Light a candle (or a bag of Flamin' Hot Cheetos, safely, please), hold your to-do list aloft, and declare, "I release you to the void of capitalist nonsense!" Then shred it, burn it (safely!), or just shove it under the couch with that one sock you'll never find.

- **Do Nothing, Proudly**: When thoughts like "I should be productive" creep in, laugh maniacally, grab a spoon, and eat cereal straight from the box. You're not avoiding work—you're communing with the eternal NOW, baby.

Handling the Time Police

The world is full of productivity bros and calendar cops who'll try to shame you for not "seizing the day." Your boss asks why you missed a deadline? Channel the serenity of a sloth on a spa day and say, "I was practicing radical presence in the eternal NOW, and your email didn't vibe with my aura." Your mom nags you about "wasting time"? Hit her with, "I'm deconstructing the illusion of linear time, Mom. It's quantum. Google it." And if your Type-A friend with a color-coded planner tries to lecture you, just blink slowly and whisper, "I'm living in a dimension where 'urgent' doesn't exist. Catch up."

For extra flair, carry a single Post-it note that says "Be" in glitter pen. When anyone questions your lack of hustle, whip it out, point to it dramatically, and walk away like you just dropped a mic. They'll be too confused to argue, and you'll be halfway to the couch before they recover.

The Cosmic Starter Pack for Time Rebels

To fully embrace the "time isn't real" lifestyle, you need minimal gear—because effort is the enemy:

- **A Couch or Bed**: Your throne of rebellion, preferably with a stain you've named (shoutout to Greg, the splotch that's seen your darkest cereal binges).

- **A Snack Stash**: Cereal, chips, or that rogue granola bar you found under the cushion. Time rebels need fuel, and chewing is basically activism.

- **A Blank Stare**: Practice looking like you're pondering the meaning of life when you're really just wondering if you can nap without spilling your coffee.

- **A Fake Planner**: Keep one for show, but fill it with entries like "Stare at Wall (2-4 p.m.)" or "Exist Loudly (All Day)." It's your decoy for the productivity police.

You Are Not a Checkbox

You are not your productivity, your inbox, or that one task you've been "meaning to do" since 2022. You are stardust and sass, wrapped in a cozy blanket of radical noncompliance, flipping the bird to a world that thinks "busy" is a personality trait. Time is fake, to-do lists are fanfic, and you're the main character in a story where "doing nothing" is the plot twist of the century.

So breathe, be, and let the universe sort out its own chaos. If anyone asks what you did today, give them a wise, slightly unhinged smile and say, "Absolutely nothing, and it was divine.

Also, I renamed my Roomba 'Guru Dave,' and we're working on our chakras." Then saunter off, ideally with a cereal crumb stuck to your shirt for maximum zen cred. You're not just living; you're a time-defying, list-ditching legend. Namaste, you chaotic, non-doing icon.

Zen Six

Existential Dread, But Make It Cozy

Congratulations, You're Spiraling Into the Void with a Throw Pillow and a Snack

Picture this: you're just chilling, maybe sipping lukewarm tea that tastes like regret and chamomile, when— *WHAM*—the universe decides to yeet an existential crisis straight into your soul. It's not a gentle nudge; it's a rogue IKEA shelf collapsing under the weight of your emotional baggage, leaving you buried in questions like "What even is all this?" and "Why am I here?" Welcome to existential dread, the emotional equivalent of your browser crashing with 43 tabs open, all of them screaming, "You're not enough, and also, where's your phone charger?" Congrats, you're officially paying attention—which, let's be honest, is your first and only mistake.

But hold up: this isn't a breakdown. It's a *breakthrough*, or at least a break-from-trying-to-figure-it-all-out. And here's the secret nobody's overpriced life coach will tell you: existential dread is way more manageable when you slap on some fuzzy socks, crank the fairy lights, and stop treating it like a TED Talk from Satan's community college. You don't need to conquer the void. You don't need to understand it. You just need to get *cozy* with it, like it's an old friend who shows up unannounced with bad vibes and a questionable haircut. Grab a blanket, dim the lights, and turn your cosmic meltdown into a vibe so snug it could star in a Pinterest board called "Apocalypse, But Make It Hygge."

The Cozy Crisis Protocol

Here's how to transform your existential spiral into a full-blown cozy zen flex, no guru or $300 retreat required:

- **Set the Mood**: Dim the lights to "emotional unraveling but make it ambiance." Flick on that Himalayan salt lamp (shoutout to Gerald, the glowy MVP who's seen your worst nights). If you've got fairy lights, tangle them up for authenticity: perfection is the enemy of dread.

- **Armor Up**: Grab a blanket so heavy it could crush your will to fight fate or at least make you forget you have an inbox. Bonus points if it's got cat hair and smells like "I haven't done laundry since Mercury went retrograde."

- **Scent the Scene**: Light a candle that smells like "forest therapy," "capitalism detox," or "I'm fine, just leave me alone." If you don't have a candle, a bag of Flamin' Hot Cheetos will do—just open it dramatically and call it "aromatherapy for rebels."

- **Breathe or Sigh**: Take a lazy breath, or just let out a dramatic sigh that says, "I'm one bad vibe away from moving to a yurt." Both are valid, and sighing burns like three calories, so it's basically cardio.

- **Snack for Stability**: Keep a stash of Goldfish crackers or half a granola bar you found under the couch. Existential dread hits different when you're crunching through your feelings.

Now, lie back on your couch (or sprawl on the floor like a starfish who's just quit its day job) and ask yourself the Big Questions:
- "Do I really want to be productive, or was that just a fever dream induced by too much coffee?"

- "Is time real, or just a scam cooked up by Big Calendar to sell me more planners?"

- "If the universe is infinite, why does my Wi-Fi suck and my Roomba keep getting stuck under the couch?"

Here's the kicker: *you don't need answers*. That's the trap, the cosmic clickbait that keeps philosophers up at night and wellness influencers in business. Enlightenment is overrated. Peace is just you, a fuzzy blanket, and a whispered, "Not today, void," as you snuggle deeper into your chaos nook. You're not lost; you're *lounging intentionally*, and that's the coziest rebellion of all.

The Cozy Dread Starter Pack

To master the art of cozy existential dread, you need minimal gear because effort is the enemy of enlightenment:
- **A Blanket Fortress**: Pile on every throw blanket you own until you're cocooned like a burrito of existential resilience. Bonus if one smells like "cozy" and "that time you spilled kombucha."

- **Fuzzy Socks**: Preferably ones with cats or tacos on them, because nothing says "I'm facing the abyss" like novelty footwear.

- **A Snack Stash**: Goldfish, Cheetos, or that rogue chocolate bar you hid from your roommate. Crunching is therapy, and crumbs are just glitter for your soul.

- **A Candle or Gerald**: If Gerald the Salt Lamp isn't available, any light source that screams "I'm sensitive but also unemployed" will do.

- **A Journal (Optional)**: For jotting down unhinged thoughts like "Am I a simulation?" or "Why does my cat stare at walls?" If writing feels like too much, just doodle a sad cloud—it's the same vibe.

Handling the Void Police

The world is full of buzzkills who'll try to drag you out of your cozy crisis. Your Type A friend with a bullet journal will lecture you about "journaling through the pain." Your mom will call and ask why you're "moping" instead of "living your potential." Some wellness bro on Instagram will try to sell you a $99 "Overcome Existential Dread" webinar. Shut. It. Down. Channel the serenity of a sloth who's just discovered edibles and say, "I'm not moping; I'm curating a cozy dialogue with the void. It's a spiritual thing, Karen." Then wrap yourself tighter in your blanket burrito and go back to contemplating whether your Roomba is sentient.

If someone really pushes, whip out a passive-aggressive affirmation like, "I am enough, even if I never figure out how to fold a fitted sheet or why my life feels like a low-budget sci-fi flick." For extra flair, light your "capitalism detox" candle mid-conversation and wave it like you're banishing their productivity vibes. They'll back off, and you'll be free to spiral in peace.

Cozy Dread Is the Ultimate Zen

Let the philosophers churn out 900-page treatises on the meaning of life. Let the influencers peddle their "find your purpose" retreats. You? You're surviving the abyss by turning it into a reading nook with fairy lights and a half-finished knitting project you'll never complete (RIP, sad scarf). That's not just resilience; that's *Zen*, baby! You're not wrestling with the void; you're cuddling it, feeding it Goldfish, and asking if it wants to watch *Nailed It!* reruns.

So the next time the meaning of life tries to jump-scare you at 3 a.m., don't panic. Grab your fuzzy socks, pile on the blankets, and lean into the dread like it's an old friend who owes you money. You're not lost; you're lounging with intention, snacking through the apocalypse, and thriving in your cozy little chaos nook. Namaste, you dread-embracing, blanket-hugging, void-vibing legend.

Zen Seven

Becoming One with the Carpet

Face-Planting Your Way to Enlightenment, One Crumb at a Time

There comes a moment in every seeker's journey when the meditation app starts sounding like a passive-aggressive life coach, the incense gives you a headache that smells like "patchouli regret," and the inner peace you're chasing is lost somewhere between the fridge and last Tuesday's existential crisis. This is when you surrender; not to a guru, not to a yoga retreat, but to the ultimate spiritual sanctuary: *the carpet*. You don't walk to your bed. You don't flop on the couch. You go full starfish, face-down, arms splayed, cheek-to-fiber, embracing the floor like it's your long-lost soulmate. Welcome to the sacred art of becoming one with the carpet, the laziest, most profound act of doing f*ckng nothing since you "forgot" to answer your boss's Slack ping.

This isn't a cry for help; it's a *spiritual practice*, a radical rebellion against a world that expects you to "seize the day" when you'd rather seize a nap. You're not "having a breakdown"; you're *melting into the fibers of existence*, achieving horizontal enlightenment so pure it could make a Himalayan monk jealous. You're flat on the floor because the world is too much, your inbox is a war zone, and also because gravity is free and nobody's Venmo-requesting you for it. This is you, opting out of life's chaos and into the fuzzy, slightly musty embrace of your carpet, which, let's be real, has seen you through worse meltdowns than this.

The Ritual of Radical Floor-Flopping

There's no posture to perfect here, no "box breathing" or "lotus pose" nonsense. Just you, the carpet, and the distant hum of a life you're currently ghosting harder than you ghosted that Tinder match who texted "wyd?" at 2 a.m. Here's how to become one with the carpet like a true Zen slacker:

- **Find Your Sacred Surface**: Any carpet will do, but bonus points if it's got a mysterious stain you've named (shoutout to Greg, the splotch that's been with you through three apartments). No carpet? A rug, bathmat, or even that one yoga mat you bought for "self-improvement" and now use as a snack crumb collector works fine.

- **Flop with Intention**: Don't just fall; *commit*. Go face-down, arms out, like you're hugging the Earth after a bad breakup. Let a stray crumb press into your cheek; it's a badge of honor, like a Zen warrior's battle scar.

- **Embrace the Void**: Feel the carpet's fibers against your skin. Smell the faint whiff of "last week's spilled kombucha." Hear the muffled chaos of your neighbor's leaf blower or your cat plotting your demise. This is your safe space, your vibe temple, your *carpet ashram*.

- **Let Thoughts Drift**: Your brain might try to ruin the vibe with thoughts like "Did I pay my electric bill?" or "Why do I own so many reusable straws?" Let them float away like bad Wi-Fi signals. You're not here to analyze; you're here to *horizontalize*.

- **Optional Moan:** If you feel a wave of existential dread or the faint memory of a childhood raisin incident, let out a soft, dramatic moan. It's like a mantra, but for people who've given up.

This isn't laziness; it's *grounded presence*, so literal you're basically part of the architecture. You're so present you could be listed on the lease as "Floor Fixture." A stray Cheeto dust on your forehead? That's your third eye's glitter. A carpet burn on your elbow? A sacred tattoo from the Church of Nope.

Handling the Carpet Critics

The world is full of buzzkills who'll try to drag you off your carpet nirvana. Your roommate barges in and asks, "Are you okay?" Channel the serenity of a sloth who's just discovered edibles and mumble, "I'm doing deep work, Karen. Google it." If they persist, roll slightly to the left, moan like you're auditioning for a zombie movie, and watch them flee in confusion. If your mom calls and demands to know why you're "lying on the floor like a toddler," hit her with, "I'm communing with the Earth's core, Mom. It's quantum. Look it up." Then hang up and nuzzle deeper into your carpet's musty embrace.

For extra flair, keep a single crystal nearby (any rock will do, even that shiny one you found in a parking lot). If someone questions your floor-flopping, point to it and whisper, "It's guiding my journey." They'll back off, terrified of your unhinged vibe, and you'll be free to spiral in peace.

The Carpet Communion Starter Pack

To master this floor-bound enlightenment, you need minimal gear because effort is the enemy:

- **A Carpet or Rug**: Preferably one with crumbs or a stain named Greg. No carpet? A bathmat or that one towel you "meant to wash" works too.

- **A Blanket (Optional)**: For draping over your legs if you want to look like a tragic poet mid-revelation. Bonus if it's got cat hair.

- **A Snack Stash**: A rogue Goldfish cracker or a half-eaten granola bar within arm's reach. Enlightenment tastes better with crumbs.

- **A Vibe**: Just show up as your messy, floor-hugging self. The carpet doesn't care if you haven't showered since Tuesday.

- **A Moan Soundtrack**: Practice a low, soulful groan that says, "I'm one bad vibe away from moving to a yurt."

The Zen of Floor-Flopping

When you finally peel yourself off the carpet, cheek creased, hair dusted with mystery fluff, slightly less like a scream trapped in a human suit, you may not have solved world hunger or your dishes problem. But you'll feel *different*. Lighter. Like you've high-fived the universe and told it, "Not today, chaos." You've communed with the floor, merged with the fibers, and reminded yourself that doing nothing is the most radical act in a world that demands you "lean in" when you'd rather lean face-down into a shag rug.

So the next time life's chaos tries to jump-scare you, don't reach for a meditation app or a self-help book. Hit the floor, hug the carpet, and let the crumbs guide your soul. You're not having a breakdown; you're having a *breakthrough*, one face-plant at a time. Namaste, you carpet-clinging, horizontal-healing legend.

Zen Eight

Daydreaming as a Divine Right

Staring Into Space Like a Blissed-Out Goldfish Is Your Cosmic Birthright

Somewhere along the line, some joyless suit, probably rocking a Bluetooth headset and chugging a Red Bull while speed-walking to a "synergy meeting," decided that staring off into space like a blissed-out goldfish was a crime against productivity. That person was wrong. Dead wrong. Probably hasn't had a good daydream since 1997, when they last imagined owning a Tamagotchi empire. They're out there, dehydrated and miserable, muttering about "time management" while the rest of us are mentally sword-fighting pirates on a glittery moonlit lake. Let's set the record straight: daydreaming isn't laziness—it's a *spiritual calling*, a sacred middle finger to the tyranny of hustle culture, and quite possibly the closest you'll ever get to enlightenment without quitting your job and moving to a yurt.

Daydreaming is your brain's VIP lounge, a mental hammock where you swing gently, unbothered, while imaginary you lives your best life: running a goat farm with a mysterious past, mastering the cello in a single afternoon, or flirting so flawlessly with a fictional barista that even your cat is impressed. This isn't wasting time; it's *healing*, a full-body rebellion against a world that screams "optimize!" while you're busy picturing yourself as a time-traveling poet with a pet velociraptor named Gerald. The hustle crowd can keep their spreadsheets; you're too busy riding a giant swan across a cosmic lagoon in your mind, and honestly, that's the most centered you've felt since you accidentally napped through a Zoom call.

Why Daydreaming Is Basically Therapy

We've been fed the lie that zoning out is "zoning away" from responsibility, but what if it's *zoning in*—into creativity, intuition, and that glorious corner of your brain that isn't traumatized by traffic or haunted by an email titled "Just Circling Back"? When you're daydreaming, you're not slacking; you're building neural highways to joy, weirdness, and the life you forgot you wanted, like one where you're a world-renowned astrophysicist who also owns a taco truck shaped like a dragon. Science says daydreaming boosts problem-solving and reduces stress, but let's be real: you don't need a study to know that imagining yourself as a benevolent monarch with a closet full of velvet capes feels better than answering your boss's Slack ping about "Q3 deliverables."

Daydreaming is your divine right, a brain spa where the only rule is "no spreadsheets allowed." It's where you process deep truths, like "Why do I own so many reusable straws?" or "What if my Roomba is secretly judging my life choices?" It's where you rehearse your Oscar acceptance speech for a film that doesn't exist, thank your nonexistent agent, and shade your high school bully in front of an imaginary audience of millions. And the best part? Nobody can evict you from this mental paradise: not your landlord, not your inbox, not even that one coworker who keeps asking if you're "free for a quick chat."

The Daydreamer's Guide to Doing Nothing

Ready to reclaim your right to wander? Here's how to daydream like a Zen slacker pro:

- **Find Your Portal**: Stare out a window with the intensity of a Nobel Prize-winning physicist who's just discovered the theory of vibes. No window? The back of your eyelids or a particularly inspiring ceiling stain (shoutout to Greg, the splotch that's seen your darkest cereal binges) works too.

- **Go Big or Go Home**: Picture yourself as a time-traveling pirate queen with a talking parrot sidekick or a reclusive artist living in a treehouse with a pet alpaca named Dolores. The weirder, the better—realism is for suckers.

- **Script Your Glory**: Mentally write an Oscar speech for your nonexistent biopic, "Couch Potato to Cosmic Legend." Thank your cat, your Roomba, and "all the haters who said I'd never nap my way to greatness."

- **Savor the Absurd**: Imagine you're fluent in Italian, wowing a fictional café with your order for "un espresso, per favore," or that you're leading a revolution of sentient houseplants against Big Lawn Mower. No limits, just vibes.

- **Keep It Secret**: Don't explain your daydreams to anyone. They don't deserve to know about your imaginary alpaca farm or your sword fight with a space kraken. It's sacred, like a diary you'd rather burn than let your mom read.

Handling the Daydream Haters

The world is crawling with productivity cops who'll try to shame you for "spacing out." Your boss catches you staring blankly during a meeting? Channel the serenity of a sloth on a spa day and say, "I was workshopping my creative vision in the astral plane. It's a process, Karen." Your mom nags you for "daydreaming instead of adulting"? Hit her with, "I'm curating a mental utopia, Mom. It's quantum. Google it." And if some wellness bro in a $200 tracksuit tells you to "focus," just smile, point to an imaginary horizon, and whisper, "I'm too busy ruling a moonlit kingdom in my mind to deal with your vibe-killing nonsense."

For extra flair, keep a notebook nearby and doodle a single, cryptic word like "Destiny" or "Velociraptor" mid-conversation. When someone asks what you're doing, sigh dramatically and say, "Capturing a vision from the ether." They'll back off, terrified of your unhinged energy, and you'll be free to resume your mental swan ride across the cosmic lagoon.

The Daydreamer's Starter Pack

To master the art of divine daydreaming, you need minimal gear because effort is the enemy:

- **A Stare-Worthy Spot**: A window, a ceiling, or that one wall with a crack you've named "The Rift to Narnia." Anywhere you can zone out without being bothered.

- **A Comfy Throne**: Couch, bed, or that one armchair with a permanent butt imprint. Bonus points if it's got crumbs spelling out "YOLO" in snack residue.

- **A Snack Stash**: Goldfish crackers or a rogue granola bar wedged between cushions. Daydreams hit different with a side of crunch.

- **A Blank Stare**: Practice looking like you're solving the meaning of life when you're really just wondering if you could train your cat to fetch beer.

- **A Vibe**: Just show up as your messy, dreamy self. Your brain's ready to throw a party, and reality's not invited.

Daydream Like Nobody's Judging

Daydreaming isn't just a pastime; it's *activism*, a glorious rebellion against a world that thinks "busy" is a personality trait. Every time you zone out, you're telling capitalism to shove its to-do lists where the sun don't shine. You're not spacing out; you're *spacing in*, diving headfirst into a mental wonderland where you're the hero, the sidekick, and the dragon all at once. So keep drifting, you radiant, mind-wandering legend. Keep riding that giant swan across your moonlit lake. And if anyone asks what you're doing, give them a wise, slightly unhinged smile and say, "Reclaiming my divine right to wander. Also, I just won an imaginary Oscar for napping."

You're not just daydreaming; you're rewriting reality, one unhinged fantasy at a time. Namaste, you goldfish-staring, alpaca-riding, cosmic-wandering icon.

Zen Nine

THE UNIVERSE DOESN'T CARE IF YOU FOLD THE LAUNDRY

Your Socks Aren't Judging You, and Neither Is the Cosmos

Picture this: out there in the cosmic wilds, a neutron star is spinning 700 times a second like it's auditioning for a galactic rave. Galaxies are smashing into each other like drunk drivers at a cosmic intersection. Planets are being born, swallowed, and probably arguing with their suns about curfew. And here you are, melting into your couch like a spiritually exhausted popsicle, crushed under the existential weight of... a pile of unfolded towels that's been staring you down since last Tuesday. Spoiler alert: the universe doesn't give a single interstellar crap about your laundry, and neither should you.

Let's get real: your laundry isn't sentient. Those socks aren't whispering, "You're a failure," in the group chat. That mountain of t-shirts on your chair, let's call it Mount Wrinkle, hasn't formed a homeowners' association to judge your life choices. The universe, in all its vast, unbothered glory, is too busy throwing black holes at each other to care whether you've paired your gym socks or if your bath towel's been living its best life as a floor mat. That guilt spiral you're riding? It's not cosmic; it's just capitalism gaslighting you into thinking your worth is tied to lint-free surfaces and color-coded closets.

The Spiritual Plot Twist

Here's the Zen bombshell: your unfolded laundry isn't a failure; it's a *revelation*. It's proof you're not a robot programmed to churn through checklists like a soulless Roomba (shoutout to Guru Dave, the one stuck under your couch). You're a being with limbs, lungs, and maybe a mild vendetta against dryer sheets that make your clothes smell like "ocean breeze" but feel like regret. That pile of clothes is a monument to your humanity, a wrinkled middle finger to a world that says you're only valuable when your socks are mated and your towels are folded into perfect, Instagram-worthy squares.

So let it pile, you radiant slacker. Let Mount Wrinkle grow so tall it casts a shadow over your productivity guilt. Let your t-shirts become crumpled metaphors for your chaotic soul. Let your unmatched socks form long-term, codependent relationships in the laundry basket, whispering sweet nothings like, "We don't need a pair to be whole." And while they're out there living their best, unpaired lives, reclaim your divine right to rest, to breathe, to stare blankly at the wall and wonder if your cat's side-eye means he's plotting to steal your snacks. This isn't laziness; it's *liberation*, a sacred act of doing fckng nothing in a world that demands you do everything.

The Laundry Liberation Protocol

Ready to tell your laundry basket to shove it? Here's your lazy-zen guide to embracing the chaos:
- **Befriend Mount Wrinkle**: Give your laundry pile a name (Greg the Stain's cousin, perhaps?) and treat it like a quirky roommate who pays rent in vibes. "Sup, Mount

Wrinkle, you're looking extra disheveled today."

- **Reframe the Chaos**: Those unmatched socks? They're practicing radical self-acceptance. That towel on the floor? It's a minimalist art installation called "Screw Folding." Your laundry isn't a chore; it's a vibe.

- **Do Nothing, Proudly**: When guilt creeps in about "wasting time," laugh like a villain in a B-movie, grab a bag of Goldfish, and sprawl on the couch. You're not avoiding chores—you're communing with the eternal NOW, baby.

- **Optional Ritual**: If you must interact with your laundry, toss one sock into the washer and call it "a ceremonial cleanse." Then walk away, commitment is overrated.

Handling the Laundry Police

The world is full of productivity cops who'll try to shame you for your laundry anarchy. Your Type-A roommate barges in, clutching their color-coded chore chart? Channel the serenity of a sloth on a spa day and say, "I'm practicing radical non-attachment to folded fabrics. It's a spiritual thing, Karen." Your mom calls and asks why your apartment looks like a thrift store explosion? Hit her with, "I'm deconstructing the illusion of domestic perfection, Mom. It's quantum. Google it." And if your coworker with a bullet journal lectures you about "time management," smile, point to an imaginary horizon, and whisper, "My laundry pile is my guru, and it's teaching me to let go."

For extra flair, keep a single, unpaired sock in your pocket. When someone questions your disheveled vibe, pull it out, wave it like a Zen talisman, and say, "This sock is my reminder that the universe doesn't care, and neither do I." They'll back off, terrified of your unhinged energy, and you'll be free to flop back onto your couch and vibe with Mount Wrinkle.

The Laundry Liberation Starter Pack

To master the art of not giving a damn about laundry, you need minimal gear because effort is the enemy:

- **A Couch Throne**: Your base for ignoring Mount Wrinkle, preferably with a stain named Greg and crumbs spelling out "YOLO" in snack residue.

- **A Snack Stash**: Goldfish, Cheetos, or that rogue granola bar you found under the cushion. Laundry rebels need fuel, and crunching is activism.

- **A Blank Stare**: Practice looking like you're pondering the cosmos when you're really wondering if you can wear the same sweatpants for the third day in a row.

- **A Fake Chore Chart**: Keep one for show, but fill it with tasks like "Befriend Sock (10 a.m.)" or "Nap to Honor Chaos (All Day)." It's your decoy for the productivity police.

- **A Vibe**: Just show up as your messy, laundry-ignoring self. Mount Wrinkle is ready to meet you where you're at.

The Universe Loves Your Mess

The universe doesn't care if your laundry is folded, your socks are paired, or your towels are living their best life as a floor rug. It's too busy spinning neutron stars and yeeting asteroids to keep score of your domestic game. If the cosmos cares about anything (and that's a big if), it's that you're still here—breathing, vibing, existing in all your gloriously disheveled glory. You're not your laundry, your checklists, or that one email you've been ghosting since last week. You're stardust and sass, wrapped in a hoodie you definitely didn't wash, and that's more than enough.

So let Mount Wrangler grow. Let your socks stage a revolution. Keep breathing, keep lounging, and keep telling the universe, "I'm here, I'm messy, and I'm thriving." If anyone asks what you did today, give them a wise, slightly unhinged smile and say, "I liberated my soul from the tyranny of folding. Also, I named my laundry pile Greg, and we're tight." Then saunter off, ideally with a Cheeto crumb stuck to your sleeve for maximum zen cred. Namaste, you laundry-defying, couch-hugging legend.

Zen Ten

Overthinking Is Just Advanced Sitting

Congratulations, You're a Mental Gymnast with a Black Belt in Spiral

While the world's Type-A overachievers are out there running marathons at dawn, chugging kale smoothies like they're auditioning for a juicer infomercial, and "crushing it" before the rest of us have even found the snooze button, you've ascended to a higher, messier plane of existence: *Advanced Sitting*™. This isn't your grandma's sitting—oh no. This is the kind where you're so still, so Zen, so fused with your couch that even your cat's like, "Did they just become furniture?" Meanwhile, your brain's throwing a full-on TED Talk nobody RSVP'd to, complete with a PowerPoint of your top ten existential crises and a Q&A about that awkward thing you said in 2016. They call it overthinking. We call it *Olympic-grade mental multitasking*, and you, my friend, are the gold-medal champ.

You're not anxious; you're just flexing a black belt in cognitive chaos. In one glorious hour of doing sweet fckng nothing, you've mentally rehearsed twelve versions of tomorrow's small talk with your neighbor (all ending in disaster), rehashed that middle school argument you *know* you lost, pictured yourself getting fired, promoted, and maybe knighted by a random monarch, and still had bandwidth to wonder if that weird car noise last week means it's secretly a Transformer plotting your doom. And all this without twitching a muscle? That's not a meltdown; that's *peak stillness*, the kind of zen that makes meditation apps clutch their digital pearls and sob.

The Scenic Route to Nowhere

Those smug mindfulness apps keep droning on about "clearing your mind" like it's a sketchy browser history you can just wipe clean. But why go blank when your brain's offering a deluxe *scenic route* through the wilds of your psyche? We're talking pit stops at Hypothetical Doom Station, Romantic Regret Rest Area, and that creepy gas station where you're pretty sure you left your self-respect back in 2012. Your mind doesn't do "empty"; it does *adventure*, careening through mental backroads like "What If I'm Secretly a Failure?" and "Did I Lock the Door in an Alternate Universe?" You're not spiraling—you're *exploring*, a fearless cartographer of your own unhinged imagination.

So sit there, you beautiful mess. Let your thoughts sprint laps like caffeinated hamsters on a wheel. You're not broken. You're not failing. You're staging a one-person Broadway show in your skull—dramatic monologues, zero costume changes, and an intermission that never happens because your brain's too busy auditioning for *Chaos: The Musical*. That's not a glitch; it's *art*, a mental masterpiece that'd make even the chillest guru go, "Whoa, that's next-level."

The Overthinker's Guide to Doing Nothing

Ready to turn your overthinking into a spiritual flex? No yoga mat or overpriced sound bath required. Here's your slacker-zen playbook:

- **Find Your Throne**: Pick a couch, bed, or that chair with your butt groove etched into it. Extra cred if it's got snack crumbs spelling out "SEND HELP."

- **Assume the Position**: Sit or flop so still that your dog thinks you've transcended. Bonus: toss a blanket over yourself like a melodramatic ghost.

- **Unleash the Chaos**: Close your eyes (or stare at the ceiling like it's spilling secrets) and let your brain off its leash. Watch it bolt through gems like "What if I accidentally Venmo'd my boss a heart emoji?" or "Is my toaster sentient and mad at me?"

- **Lean Into the Weird**: Go full absurd. Picture yourself as a time-traveling pirate with a pet parrot that only squawks conspiracy theories, or a wizard who forgot the spell for "calm the hell down."

- **No Judgment Allowed**: If your brain tries guilting you for "wasting time," cackle like a supervillain and yell, "This is mental cardio, baby! I'm shredded up here!"

When the Thought Police Come Knocking

The world's full of productivity narcs ready to bust you for "overthinking." Boss catches you zoning out in a meeting? Flash a sloth-on-vacation grin and say, "I'm curating genius in the ether, Dave. Catch up." Mom nags about "daydreaming"? Hit her with, "I'm designing a mental empire, Ma. It's quantum-level stuff; look it up." And if some yoga bro in a $300 tank top tells you to "just meditate," smirk, tap your temple, and whisper, "I'm too busy scripting my Nobel acceptance speech for Overthinking Excellence to vibe with your basic-ass advice."

For max chaos, keep a notebook handy and jot down a random word like "Fate" or "Pterodactyl" mid-chat. When they ask, sigh deeply and mutter, "It's a vision from the void." They'll flee, and you'll reign supreme in your spiral kingdom.

Your Overthinking Starter Kit

Mastering *Advanced Sitting*™ takes zero effort; perfect, right? Here's what you need:

- **A Comfy Spot**: Couch, bed, or that rug you impulse-bought because it "spoke to you." Crumbs are a vibe.

- **Snacks**: Stale Goldfish or a granola bar you forgot about. Overthinking's better with crunch.

- **A Dead-Eyed Stare**: Look like you're decoding the universe when you're really just wondering if your cat's plotting a coup.

- **Your Messy Self**: No prep needed. Your brain's already RSVP'd to the chaos party.

Overthinking: The Ultimate Spiritual Win

When you finally peel yourself off the couch, bleary-eyed and clueless about where the last hour went, don't sweat it. That wasn't wasted time; that was *spiritual cross-training*. Your mind took a globe-trotting jaunt (passport pending), your body chilled harder than a monk on a mountaintop, and your laundry sat there like a proud shrine to your dedication to doing f*cking nothing. You didn't fix climate change or your sink full of dishes, but you *did* imagine yourself as a knighted poet, a rogue detective, and maybe a talking taco. That's not overthinking—that's *overwinning*.

So keep sitting, you glorious, spiral-loving legend. Let your brain run wild while your body vibes like a Zen pro. You're not just overthinking; you're rewriting reality, one bonkers thought at a time. Namaste, you couch-bound visionary, you mental gymnast supreme.

Zen Eleven

SCROLLING WITH AWARENESS (AND LOW EXPECTATIONS)

Namaste, You Glorious, Algorithm-Chasing Disaster

Oh, doomscrolling, humanity's oldest tradition, handed down from the days when your grandma thought "LOL" meant "Lots of Love" and used it in condolence texts. You sit. You swipe. You forget sunlight's a thing and that your eyes are supposed to blink, not just glaze over like a pair of sad, digital donuts. But hold up, here's the galaxy-brain revelation: you *can* turn this soul-sucking habit into a spiritual rager! Namaste, you chaotic, screen-obsessed gremlin—enlightenment's just one unhinged TikTok away!

This ain't about ditching your scroll game (please, we both know that's not happening). It's about *cranking it up*, transforming your endless thumb-flicking into a mindful, laugh-out-loud party so wild, even your phone's dying battery will salute you. You're not wasting time; you're mastering *Scrolling Awareness*™, a next-level flex that makes yoga retreats look like a snooze fest. So grab your cracked-screen lifeline, flop onto your crumb-covered couch, and let's scroll like zen slackers on a mission to nowhere!

The Sacred Scroll: Your Guide to Digital Nirvana

Here's how to turn your doomscrolling into a spiritual joyride: no incense, no overpriced leggings, just pure, unfiltered chaos:

Step One: Pick Your Digital Dumpster Fire

Fire up your app of choice: Instagram for the filtered flexing, TikTok for the brain-cell-killing dance trends, or Craigslist Missed Connections if you're ready to spiritually bond with "Guy in Neon Flip-Flops at Gas Station." It's all the same glorious mess, just with different vibes of unhinged.

Step Two: Breathe in the Absolute Madness

Take a deep, dramatic breath, like you're about to dive into a pool of Wi-Fi signals and regret. Smell the stale vibes of your unwashed hoodie and that mystery takeout container. You're not just scrolling; you're *plunging into the abyss*, and it's serving up influencers doing downward dog on a yacht.

Step Three: Feast Your Eyes on the Freakshow

Behold the magic: a fitness bro guzzling neon kale juice while yelling about "gut vibes," a raccoon pulling off a pizza heist like it's *Ocean's Eleven, and* a random kid's kindergarten graduation with a gown fancier than your entire wardrobe. Feel your eyeballs shrivel into tiny, judgmental prunes. Hear your soul scream, "We used to hunt mammoths; now we're watching a parrot twerk to Lizzo!" Keep going; it's your destiny.

Step Four: Float Above the Nonsense Like a Snarky Monk

Watch your thoughts pop off like a circus of deranged clowns: "Why is this dude screaming about probiotics like he's curing world hunger?" "How did my ex level up to hot *and* insufferable?" "Is this a bot or just a human who's lost the plot?" Let it all drift by like a bad signal in a storm. You're not here to judge—you're here to *vibe*.

Step Five: Let Go… But Not Really

Sure, "release the judgment," like the meditation gurus say, but keep scrolling, because quitting's for quitters, and that viral video of a llama doing karate isn't gonna watch itself. Productivity? Inner peace? Nah, you're too busy chasing the next dopamine hit.

Step Six: Salute the Chaos and Bounce

When your thumb's screaming for mercy or you've accidentally followed a shirtless gym rat with a PhD in protein shakes, it's time to wrap it up. Give your phone a half-hearted bow (or just flip it the bird), mutter, "I honor the chaos," and yeet yourself off the app. Boom—enlightenment unlocked. Maybe.

Your Scroll Survival Kit

To dominate this digital Zen game, you don't need much; effort's for suckers:

- **A Phone**: Bonus points if the screen's cracked enough to look like modern art.

- **A Throne**: Couch, bed, or that one chair you've basically merged with. Crumbs optional but encouraged.

- **Snacks**: Stale pretzels, a rogue M&M from last month, or anything with crunch to fuel the scroll.

- **A Blank Stare**: Look like you're solving life's mysteries when you're really just wondering if that influencer's handstand is CGI.

- **Zero Hopes**: Keep expectations so low they're basically chilling in the Earth's core. You're not here for wisdom—you're here for *vibes*.

Shutting Down the Scroll Haters

Got some productivity cop trying to shame your scroll sesh? Hit 'em with these:

- **Boss on Zoom**: "Sorry, Karen, I'm channeling the digital ether for inner growth. You wouldn't get it."

- **Naggy Mom**: "Ma, I'm tapping into the collective soul of the internet. It's, like, cosmic."

- **Smug Unplugger**: Smirk, pat your phone, and say, "I'm too busy riding the algorithm wave to deal with your 'touch grass' TED Talk." Pro tip: Scribble "Fate" or "Squirrel" in a notebook mid-scroll, then sigh like you've seen the future. They'll back off, and you'll look like a chaotic prophet.

Scroll Hard, Win at Life

When you finally peel your crusty eyes from the screen, half-dead but cackling, you haven't wasted an hour. You've *leveled up*. Your brain's been on a wild safari through the digital jungle, your thumb's ripped, and your dishes are still plotting a revolt in the sink. You didn't cure climate change, but you *did* see a dog in a tuxedo explain NFTs in barks. That's not doomscrolling; that's *doomslaying*, and it's the most fun you'll have on the path to nowhere.

So scroll on, you radiant, app-hopping rockstar. Let your mind swim in the madness while your body vibes like a zen champ. You're not just scrolling; you're rewriting the universe, one batshit post at a time. Namaste, you absolute legend!

Zen Twelve

Zen and the Art of Saying "Nope"

The Sacred "Nope": Your Spiritual Superpower, No Crystals Required

Picture this: you're standing at the edge of a chaotic abyss called "modern life," and someone's trying to shove a to-do list longer than a CVS receipt into your trembling hands. What's your move? Do you clutch some overpriced quartz, light a sage stick that smells like a forest fire's midlife crisis, or force yourself through a seven-step morning routine that demands you greet the sunrise like a motivational poster? Nah. You pull out the big guns: a simple, glorious "Nope." Two syllables, infinite power; no incense required.

"Nope" isn't just a word; it's a *spiritual superpower*. It's the ultimate boundary-setting, soul-preserving, burnout-busting mantra for anyone who's ever wanted to yeet themselves out of a group chat or a guilt trip. Crystals? Overrated. Vision boards? Extra. That juice cleanse your coworker won't shut up about? HARD NOPE with a side of "I'd rather drink my dignity." This isn't avoidance; it's *enlightened refusal*, a sacred act of saying, "My energy's too precious for your nonsense, Brenda."

When to Wield the Nope: A Survival Guide

The modern world is a gauntlet of obligations wrapped in guilt and sprinkled with FOMO glitter. But "Nope" is your shield. Here's when to deploy it:

- **The Pointless Meeting**: Your boss calls a "quick sync" that's really just a circle-jerk of buzzwords. "Nope, my calendar's booked with 'sanity preservation.'"

- **The Absurd Family Favor**: Your cousin insists you bake a gluten-free birthday cake for their dog by tomorrow. "Nooope, I'm not a pastry chef for paws."

- **The Social Trap**: A friend invites you to a "networking event" that's suspiciously pyramid-shaped. "Nope, I'd rather network with my couch cushions."

- **The Wellness Scam**: Someone pitches a detox that's just kale-flavored misery. "HARD NOPE, I'm detoxing from bad vibes, not joy."

Every time you say "yes" to these soul-suckers, you're saying "no" to yourself: your peace, your snacks, your sacred blanket burrito time. "Nope" flips the script. It's a love letter to your own damn energy.

The Nope Ritual: A Step-by-Step Guide to Zen AF Refusal

Saying "Nope" isn't just a reflex; it's an *art form*. Here's how to master it with maximum Zen and minimum effort:

1. **Tune Into Your Gut**: When someone asks you to do something, and your insides twist like you just saw pineapple on pizza, that's your signal. Your body's screaming "NOPE" louder than a toddler at naptime.

2. **Embrace Sloth Mode**: Picture yourself as a wise, chill

sloth dangling from a branch, unbothered by the dumpster fire below. Then, with the calm of someone who's just discovered Wi-Fi and sweatpants, say, "Nope."

3. **Add Drama**: Elevate your "Nope" with flair, a slow head shake, a raised hand like you're warding off a vampire, or a full-body flop onto the nearest soft surface. Extra points if you're already burrito'd in a blanket.

4. **Bask in the Afterglow**: Once the "Nope" lands, relish the silence. It's the sound of the universe nodding, "You're a badass."

The Blanket Burrito: Your Nope Fortress

Some days, the world's chaos hits like a swarm of caffeinated wasps. Your defense? The *Blanket Burrito*. Grab every quilt, throw, and that ratty afghan your grandma made, and wrap yourself into a cozy cocoon of refusal. From this fluffy fortress, you can nope out of anything: emails, laundry, the vague guilt of not "being productive" with the serenity of a monk who's traded lotus poses for Netflix. If someone knocks, mumble through the layers, "I'm in a spiritual time-out. Leave offerings of snacks and begone."

Pro tip: Stash some Goldfish or a rogue Twix bar in there. Enlightenment's better with a side of crunch.

Deflecting the Nope Naysayers

Not everyone gets the gospel of "Nope." Pushback is inevitable from the yes-addicts and hustle junkies. Your coworker whines, "Why aren't you a team player?" You reply, "I'm playing for Team Me, and we're winning at naps." Your dad grumbles, "You should get out more!" You counter, "I'm out here thriving in my blanket fort, Pops." And when some LinkedIn bro in a Patagonia vest tells you to "crush it," just smirk and say, "I'm crushing it at saying 'Nope' to your TED Talk energy."

For the persistent, keep a glitter-pen "Nope" sticky note handy. Slap it on their forehead like a Zen hex and strut away. They'll be too baffled to chase you, and you'll be free to burrito in peace.

Your Nope Essentials

To live the nope life, you don't need much; effort's the enemy, after all:

- **A Couch**: Your nope HQ, complete with a mystery stain and crumbs that spell "freedom."

- **Blankets**: Pile 'em high until you're a refusal tortilla. Smells like victory and last week's popcorn? Perfect.

- **Snacks**: Stale chips, a lint-dusted gummy bear, or whatever fuels your nope fire.

- **A Vibe**: No prep required. Your messy, glorious self is already nope-ready.

Nope, Like You Mean It

Every "yes" to something your gut hates is a betrayal of your inner slacker-sage. But every "Nope"? That's a power move, a reclaiming of your peace, a middle finger to the chaos gods. So wield it proudly, you radiant, boundary-drawing legend. Let your intuition be your guide, your couch be your shrine, and your blanket burrito be your battle gear. You're not lazy; you're a nope ninja, a discernment rockstar, a poet of "nah."

Next time someone asks what you're up to, flash a wild grin and say, "I'm doing nothing, and it's holy. Also, my couch and I are exclusive now." Then saunter off, snack crumbs trailing like a zen breadcrumb path. Namaste, you nope-slinging icon.

Zen Thirteen

GHOSTING GUILT LIKE A NINJA MONK

Vanish Like a Robe-Wearing, Sandal-Sliding Legend of Nope

There's an ancient spiritual practice no one talks about. It's not from a dusty scroll or a monastery with Wi-Fi issues; it's called *not replying to that text*. You read it. You thought about replying. You even typed "Hey! So sorry I missed this!" and then, *poof,* you vanished like a robe-wearing, sandal-sliding ninja monk of serenity. And guess what? That's not just okay; it's a *power move*. You're not a flake; you're a vibe curator, a boundary-setting badass, a ghosting guru in a world that thinks "read receipts" are a personality trait.

We live in a digital hellscape that worships immediate response like it's the 11th commandment. Reply rates are the new moral compass, and leaving someone on read is treated like you've committed a war crime against Karen's group chat. But let's get real: do you think the Buddha stressed about ghosting enlightenment three times before chilling under that tree? Hell no. He probably left the universe on "delivered" for a solid decade. And monks? They're out here dodging emails from their cave retreats like pros. You're not failing at life; you're channeling ancient wisdom in a world that's forgotten how to chill.

The Art of the Ghost: Your Guide to Enlightened Disappearance

Ghosting guilt is modern karma clutter, clinging to you like spiritual spam and whispering, "You're a bad friend/human/Yelp reviewer." But you're not. You're just a glorious mess with a nervous system on its last bar, a social battery that's been blinking red since 2019, and zero interest in RSVP-ing to a third baby shower for someone's gluten-free dog. Here's your practice for vanishing like a Zen ninja and leaving the guilt in the dust:

1. **Pause Like a Pro**: When the guilt creeps in, usually around 2 a.m., when your brain's replaying that text from your coworker's cousin's friend—stop. Place your phone face down like it's a sacred ritual. Bonus points if you sage it or yeet it into a pile of laundry.

2. **Breathe Like You Mean It**: Inhale deeply, exhale like you're blowing out the candles on your last f*ck to give. Whisper to yourself, "I am not a notification. I am a living, breathing, snack-hoarding being."

3. **Ghost with Grace**: If you must reply (and let's be honest, sometimes the vibes demand it), keep it short and unapologetic: "Got buried in life. Still love you. Also, I'm in a blanket fort now." Then vanish again. Poof. Serenity restored.

The Blanket Fort Retreat: Your Ghosting HQ

For those days when the world's demands feel like a swarm of notifications from hell, retreat to your ultimate zen sanctuary:

the *Blanket Fort*. This isn't just any fort; it's a vibe temple, a nope fortress, a sacred cocoon of refusal. Build it with every blanket, pillow, and that one hoodie you haven't washed since 2022. Inside, you're untouchable. If someone texts, let it buzz. If they call, let it ring. You're not here; you're in a spiritual chrysalis, and the only thing getting through is a rogue Cheeto you dropped last week.

Pro tip: Hang a "Do Not Disturb" sign written in glitter pen (or Sanskrit, if you're extra). If someone knocks, mumble through the blankets, "I'm in silent retreat. Leave snacks and begone." They'll think you're either enlightened or unhinged; either way, they'll leave you alone.

Guilt-Busting Mantras for the Ghosting Guru

When the ghosting guilt tries to sneak back in (and it will, because brains are jerks), arm yourself with these affirmations:

- "I am not a 24/7 customer service hotline. I am a vibe curator."

- "My energy is sacred, and Karen's potluck invite is not."

- "The Buddha ghosted enlightenment three times, and he turned out fine."

- "I don't owe anyone my Wi-Fi password or my immediate attention."

Repeat these while lounging in your fort, ideally with a snack stash of Goldfish and a playlist called "Songs to Ghost To." You're not just ghosting—you're *ascending*.

Handling the Ghost Hunters

The world is full of reply-rate cops and guilt-trippers who'll try to drag you back into the chaos. Your friend texts, "You alive?"

Your mom calls to ask why you're "avoiding everyone." Some rando from high school DMs you about their MLM pitch. Shut. It. Down. Channel your inner ninja monk and respond with serene detachment:

- **To the Concerned Friend**: "I'm alive, just in a spiritual chrysalis. Emerging soon. Maybe."

- **To the Naggy Relative**: "I'm curating my energy, Mom. It's like minimalism but for people."

- **To the MLM Pitch**: "Nope, I'm allergic to pyramid schemes and bad vibes."

For the persistent, pull out the ultimate flex: "I was deep in silent retreat... in my blanket fort. The Wi-Fi's bad there." Then vanish again, like the serene, sandal-sliding legend you are.

Your Ghosting Starter Pack

To master the art of guilt-free ghosting, you need minimal gear, because effort is the enemy:

- **A Phone on Silent**: Bonus points if it's buried under a pile of laundry or "lost" in the couch.

- **A Blanket Fort**: Your vibe HQ, complete with crumbs and a faint smell of "I haven't left in days."

- **Snacks**: Stale pretzels, a rogue Twix bar, anything that says, "I'm thriving in my chaos."

- **A Vibe**: No prep needed. Your messy, ghosting self is already a masterpiece.

Ghost Like You Mean It

Every time you reply out of guilt, you're basically Venmo-ing your peace to the chaos gods. But every time you ghost with intention, you're reclaiming your energy, one unread message at a time. So vanish proudly, you radiant, boundary-setting ninja. Let your intuition be your guide, your blanket fort be your temple, and your silence be your sermon. You're not flaky; you're a ghosting guru, a discernment deity, a poet of peaceful disappearance.

And if anyone asks why you ghosted, flash a wild grin and say, "I was deep in retreat, communing with the void. Also, my phone died, and so did my will to reply." Then saunter off, ideally with a snack crumb stuck to your sleeve for maximum zen cred. Namaste, you ghosting, guilt-slaying icon.

Zen Fourteen

Procrastination as a Portal to the Divine

Congratulations, You're a Gold-Medal Slacker with a PhD in Divine Delay

Let's be real: if procrastination were an Olympic sport, you'd be standing on the podium, draped in a robe made of unfinished to-do lists, clutching a half-eaten bag of Cheetos, and wearing a crown of crumpled Post-its that scream "I'll do it tomorrow." And guess what? You deserve gold, a parade, and maybe a nap, because you, my friend, are a procrastination *legend*. While the world's productivity cops are out there screaming "You're lazy!" and "You're avoiding responsibility!" we know the truth: procrastination isn't avoidance; it's *intuitive scheduling*, a sacred art passed down from ancient sloths and high-functioning chaos gremlins who knew that sometimes the best move is no move at all.

You weren't "wasting time"—you were letting your soul marinate in the cosmic soup of possibility. You were giving your dreams time to stretch, yawn, and maybe take a nap themselves. You were creating *negative space* around your intentions, like a zen master who's too chill to care about deadlines. And while the universe was busy rearranging your priorities, you were deep in a YouTube spiral of oddly satisfying cleaning videos, emerging 43 minutes later with zero regrets and a vague plan to maybe organize your sock drawer. That's not laziness—that's *divine delay*, baby.

The Way of the Procrastinator Monk: A Sacred Practice

In this temple of chill, procrastination is a spiritual flex, a middle finger to the cult of "crushing it." Here's how to master it like a robe-wearing, snack-hoarding sage:

1. **Begin with Purpose**: "Today, I will finally do my taxes. Or at least find the forms. Or maybe just think about where the forms are."

2. **Allow the Shift**: "But first, I need to reorganize my sock drawer. Wait, is that a loose thread? Better stare at it for 10 minutes."

3. **Enter the Vortex of Distraction**: Suddenly, you're knee-deep in a Wikipedia spiral about the mating habits of sloths. This is research for your future self—trust the process.

4. **Surrender to the Flow**: It's night. You've done nothing. You're weirdly fulfilled. That's the divine at work, whispering, "Nap first, taxes never."

5. **Embrace the Chaos**: When guilt creeps in, laugh like a supervillain and say, "I'm not avoiding—I'm aligning with the universe's timeline. It's not ready for my genius yet."

Procrastination: The Secret to Genius

Let's talk facts: some of the world's greatest ideas were born from procrastination. Newton? Dude was literally sitting under a tree, doing sweet f*ckng nothing, when gravity smacked him in the head. That's high-level chill. You're not lazy—you're *pre-enlightened*, a visionary who knows that brilliance needs space to breathe (or nap). Your brain's out here playing 4D chess while the productivity bros are stuck on level one, color-coding their planners like it's a spiritual awakening.

So next time someone says, "You're avoiding your responsibilities," channel your inner sloth sage, give them a slow blink, and whisper, "I'm not avoiding. I'm curating divine inaction. The universe will handle it. Or not. Either way, I'm good."

The Procrastination Starter Pack

To master this sacred art, you need minimal gear—because effort is the enemy:

- **A Couch with a Butt Groove**: Your throne of divine delay, complete with a stain named Greg and crumbs that spell "YOLO."

- **Snacks**: Stale pretzels, a rogue Twix bar, anything that says, "I'm thriving in my chaos."

- **A Playlist**: "Songs to Do Nothing To": Think lo-fi beats and whale sounds. Vibes only.

- **A Vibe**: No prep needed. Your messy, glorious self is already a procrastination masterpiece.

Handling the Haters

The world's full of productivity cops ready to guilt-trip your zen. Your boss asks why you missed the deadline? Say, "I was aligning with the divine timeline. The universe wasn't ready for my genius yet." Then flop onto the nearest couch and nap like a champion. Your mom nags about "wasting time"? Hit her with, "I'm practicing radical stillness, Mom. It's quantum-level chill—Google it." And if some LinkedIn bro in a Patagonia vest tells you to "optimize your workflow," smirk, point to your snack stash, and whisper, "I'm too busy optimizing my nap schedule to deal with your hustle porn."

For extra chaos, keep a notebook filled with doodles of cats and half-baked ideas. When someone questions your procrastination, flip to a random page, nod sagely, and say, "This is my vision board. It's abstract." They'll back off, and you'll be free to spiral in peace.

Procrastinate Like a Legend

Every time you put off a task, you're not just delaying; you're *ascending*. You're telling the universe, "I trust you to sort this out while I vibe with my sock drawer." So keep procrastinating, you radiant, divine-delaying legend. Let your intuition be your guide, your couch be your temple, and your snack stash be your offering. You're not lazy; you're a procrastination ninja, a stillness rockstar, a poet of "I'll do it later."

And if anyone asks what you're doing today, flash a wild grin and say, "Absolutely nothing, and it's holy. Also, I'm in a committed relationship with my couch." Then saunter off, snack crumbs trailing like a zen breadcrumb path. Namaste, you divine, nap-taking icon.

Zen Fifteen

MEDITATIVE SNACKING AND THE SACRED CRINKLE OF THE CHIP BAG

It starts with a crinkle. Not just any crinkle; the sacred rustle of a chip bag at full enlightenment volume. This isn't snacking. This is a ceremony. This is sacrament. This is spiritual surrender to processed bliss.

You think monks with bells have something on me? Please. I've got a half-empty bag of stale Doritos, a couch with the emotional support of a beanbag therapist, and a lamp that's seen some shit. And tonight, I enter snacklightenment.

Because in a world drowning in green juices and productivity podcasts, the bravest act might be to lie horizontal and stuff your face with something powdered in artificial cheese and shame. You heard me: **meditative snacking** is the new mindfulness. And I am the crunchy oracle.

The Sacred Crinkle Doctrine

Snacking isn't a vice. It's a vow. A bold rejection of spinach smoothies and hustle porn. A declaration that your soul deserves salt, crunch, and a little bit of orange powder in places it doesn't belong.

The chip bag speaks in tongues. Every rustle is a message from the snack gods:

- *You are enough.*

- *You do not need to meal prep.*

- *You may eat the broken chips first.*

- *You are forgiven for eating the whole damn bag.*

The holy trinity? Crunch. Crumbs. Cringe. All welcome at this altar.

Building Your Snackitation Station

To achieve full-body snacknosis, you'll need the proper setup. Here's your sacred starter kit:

- **The Crinkle Cloak:** A blanket that's seen every season of *The Great British Bake Off*. Preferably covered in cracker crumbs and existential dread.

- **The Snack Chalice:** Any bowl large enough to cradle your chosen vice—be it chips, cookies, or that weird off-brand cereal that tastes like regret.

- **The Crunch Mantra:** Repeat after me: *"I chew, therefore I am."*

- **The Judgmental Feline Witness:** Optional, but recommended. Cats add a level of shame so potent it actually deepens the transcendence.

The Ritual of the Chip

1. **Sit. Sprawl. Collapse.** There is no wrong posture in snackitation. All positions are valid, especially fetal.

2. **Open the bag slowly.** Let the crinkle ring through your bones. This is your conch shell. Your summoning horn. Your clarion call to inner peace.

3. **Eat with presence.** Feel the texture. Hear the crunch. Taste the void.

4. **Ignore the haters.** Someone will inevitably say, "Are you really eating that at 2 p.m. on a Tuesday?" To which you shall reply, "Yes, Cheryl. I'm healing."

5. **Receive the blessing.** You'll know you've achieved snacklightenment when you're surrounded by crumbs, hollow packaging, and the unshakable peace of someone who has truly let go.

Snacklightenment Is a Journey (Not a Diet Plan)

Look, this isn't about gluttony. This is about **reclaiming ritual**. About saying no to kale cleanses and yes to cosmic snaccidents. About the **radical power of pausing**, chewing, and letting your body be both temple and trash can.

You are not broken for wanting a Cheeto over a chia seed. You are not behind in life because you meditated with a cookie instead of an app. You are not less spiritual because you reach for crunchy serotonin instead of guided breathwork.

You are sacred. You are crunchy. You are enough, even when licking the flavor dust off your shirt.

Final Blessing of the Bag

When the crinkle fades, and the snack bag lies empty, lift your orange-dusted fingers to the sky and whisper:

Now go forth, you glorious snack mystic. Meditate through the munch.

Snack like your enlightenment depends on it, because it just might.

Zen Sixteen

How to Politely Decline Every Invitation Forever (Without Losing Friends or Your Soul)

The Noble Path of Nope: An Introduction to Guilt-Free Living

Picture this: your phone buzzes with yet another invitation: *"Hey, wanna come to my artisanal kombucha tasting slash vision board party?"* and your soul lets out a tiny, exhausted scream. You don't hate people. You don't even hate kombucha (well, maybe a little). But the idea of leaving your house, putting on real pants, and pretending to care about someone's Pinterest-inspired life goals makes you want to yeet yourself into a parallel dimension where calendars don't exist. Fear not, brave recluse, because you've stumbled upon the sacred scrolls of *Zen Sixteen*: the ultimate guide to declining every invitation forever while keeping your friendships intact and your soul as pristine as a freshly laundered hoodie.

Declining invitations isn't just a life hack; it's a lifestyle, a vibe, a full-on *aesthetic*. You're not rude; you're a curator of your own peace, a master of the polite "no" so flawless it could be embroidered on a throw pillow. This isn't about burning bridges; it's about building a moat around your personal fortress of solitude, complete with a drawbridge you only lower for pizza delivery. With the right mix of grace, humor, and strategic vagueness, you can dodge every social obligation from here to eternity without anyone suspecting you're just three episodes deep into a *Murder She Wrote* marathon.

The Commandments of Declination: Your Toolkit for Eternal Freedom

Here's how to say "no" like a pro; think of it as a cheat sheet for dodging small talk, awkward hugs, and that one friend who insists on group karaoke. Each scenario comes with a tailor-made escape plan, guaranteed to keep you cozy and uncommitted.

1. The Wedding Invitation: Because Love Is Grand, But So Is Your Couch

Weddings are beautiful—vows, tears, overpriced cake—until you realize you're shelling out $200 on a gift just to watch someone's uncle do the Macarena. Declining a wedding invite feels like a high-stakes heist, but it's doable with finesse.

- **How to Decline**: "Oh, I'm gutted I can't make it to your big day; my spirit animal's hosting a mandatory retreat that weekend. Sending you a toaster and all my love, though!"

- **Pro Tip**: Mail a gift so lavish they'll feel guilty for even wanting you there. A $30 AmazonBasics blender says, "I care," without saying, "I'll wear Spanx for you."

2. The Party Invitation: Where "Fun" Means Noise and Spilled Dip

Parties sound great until you're trapped in a corner, nodding along to someone's rant about their new juicer while guacamole congeals on your shirt. You're not a buzzkill—you're just overstimulated and under-caffeinated.

- **How to Decline**: "I'd love to rage with you, but I'm mid-cleanse: emotional, not dietary. Let's do a quiet hang soon, just us and zero decibels."

- **Pro Tip**: Offer a rain check so vague it's basically a mirage. "Soon" could mean next week or when the sun explodes—your call.

3. The Coffee Date: A Polite Interrogation Disguised as a Chat

Coffee dates are cute in theory—two pals, steaming mugs, witty banter—until you realize it's an hour of dodging questions about your "life plan" while pretending you like oat milk. Nope, not today.

- **How to Decline**: "I'm dying to catch up, but my horoscope says I'm in a 'solitude cycle.' How about a walk instead, like, next month?"

- **Pro Tip**: Suggest an alternative so low-effort they'll forget it by the time you flake again. A "walk" sounds wholesome but requires zero eye contact.

4. The Work Event: Team Bonding or Soul Erosion?

Your boss thinks a happy hour will boost morale, but you'd rather boost your morale by not listening to Dave from accounting explain cryptocurrency over warm beer. You're not a bad employee—you're just allergic to forced fun.

- **How to Decline**: "I'd be there, but I'm facilitating a personal wellness seminar that night—attendance: me, myself, and I. Cheers to the team, though!"

- **Pro Tip**: Mention "wellness" and they'll assume you're too enlightened to argue with. Bonus points if you send a cryptic Slack emoji () to seal the deal.

5. The Family Gathering: Love Them, But From Afar

Family events are a minefield—Grandma's asking why you're still single, Uncle Bob's on his third conspiracy theory, and there's always a cousin selling essential oils. You'd rather send a group text than sit through that.

- **How to Decline**: "I'm so sad to miss the chaos. I'm booked for a self-imposed grounding ritual. I'll call Grandma with all my excuses, promise!"

- **Pro Tip**: Blame something spiritual and call later with a voice so sweet they'll forgive you before the mashed potatoes go cold.

The Fine Art of Excuse Crafting: Keep 'Em Guessing

A great decline is like a magic trick: dazzle them with charm, distract with mystery, and vanish before they ask questions. Here's the formula:

- **Step 1: Flatter**: "Your event sounds like the social highlight of the decade." They're too busy blushing to notice you're bailing.

- **Step 2: Mystify**: "I'm tied up with a personal project: think less 'DIY' and more 'existential recalibration.'" Nobody's fact-checking your soul's to-do list.

- **Step 3: Deflect**: "I'd hate to show up half-present; you deserve my full sparkle!" Now they're thanking *you* for staying home.

Example in action: "Your barbecue's gonna be epic, but I'm knee-deep in a vibe reset, gotta sage my whole apartment. Catch you when my energy's less chaotic!" Boom. You're free, and they're picturing you as some incense-wielding sage instead of a snack-hoarding goblin.

Survival Gear for the Socially Reluctant

To thrive as a professional naysayer, you need props. Here's your starter kit:

- **A "Busy" Persona**: Mutter about "scheduling conflicts" like you're a celebrity dodging paparazzi.

- **A Go-To Text**: "So sorry, I'm swamped—rain check?" Short, sweet, and reusable.

- **A Decoy Hobby**: Claim you're "really into pottery now" so they think you're artsy, not antisocial.

- **A Loyal Pet**: "Can't leave Fluffy alone—she's got separation anxiety." Fluffy's a stuffed animal, but they don't need to know that.

The Zen of No: A Conclusion Worth Toasting (Alone)

Declining invitations isn't about ghosting your crew; it's about honoring your inner peace with the ferocity of a warrior monk. Every "no" is a victory lap around your living room, a high-five to your truest self, and a middle finger to the tyranny of group chats buzzing "where u at?" You're not losing friends; you're gaining *you*. And if someone's mad you skipped their paint-and-sip night, well, they'll get over it when you Venmo them $5 with a note that says, "For the rosé I didn't spill."

So go forth, you radiant hermit. Decline with gusto. Sip your tea, queue your shows, and let the world spin on without you. Your soul's not for sale, and your RSVP is forever "no"—delivered with a wink and a wave from the coziest corner of your universe.

Zen Seventeen

"Sorry, I Was Meditating", and Other Holy Lies That Work Every Damn Time

Meditation: Your Spiritual Alibi for Life's Chaos

You weren't meditating. You were sprawled on your couch, mainlining dog memes while excavating a tub of hummus with your bare hands like a raccoon in a spiritual crisis. Maybe you had a glass of rosé balanced on your stomach, or maybe you were arguing with your Wi-Fi router because it dared to buffer during a *Great British Bake Off* marathon. Point is, you were living your truth—until your phone buzzed with a call from someone expecting you to, like, *exist* in their reality. Nope. Time to deploy the ultimate weapon in your zen arsenal: "Sorry, I was meditating."

This is the spiritual equivalent of a get-out-of-jail-free card, a conversational sage bomb that clears the room of accountability. It's vague, it's lofty, it's so unimpeachably enlightened that nobody dares question it unless they want to look like they've never heard of a chakra. Drop a "Sorry, I was meditating," and watch the world bend to your whims. Missed a deadline? Meditating. Forgot to text back? Meditating. Showed up to brunch with hummus in your hair and a vibe that screams "I haven't seen sunlight in 72 hours"? *Meditating, obviously.* It's the lie that's so holy it's basically true.

The Art of the Spiritual Lie

Crafting the perfect spiritual excuse is an art form, like painting a masterpiece with incense smoke and vibes. The key is to lean into the mystical jargon so hard that people are too intimidated—or too confused—to push back. Here's your holy grail of excuses, ready to deploy at a moment's notice:

- "I was deep in a theta brainwave state, exfoliating my aura. Couldn't risk disrupting the cosmic download."

- "I transcended linear time, so I didn't realize it was 3 p.m. or, like, Tuesday. Clocks are so 3D."

- "My third eye was buffering, and I couldn't get a signal. Mercury's in retrograde, you know how it is."

- "I was channeling my inner divine feminine, and she told me to stay in bed with a bag of Flamin' Hot Cheetos."

- "I was in a sacred dialogue with my houseplant, Gerald. He's very wise but takes forever to get to the point."

If someone dares to question your excuse—say, your boss asking why you missed the 9 a.m. Zoom call—just close your eyes, inhale deeply through your nose like you're sniffing the secrets of the universe, and hold the silence. Let them marinate in their own doubt. Watch them wonder if *they're* the unenlightened one for not understanding your "journey." The lie becomes truth when you commit so hard that even you start believing you were meditating instead of Googling "why does my cat hate me."

The Performance Is the Power

To sell these holy lies, you've got to lean into the theatrics. Mid-conversation, casually light some incense and wave it around like you're warding off bad vibes (or their expectations). Bonus points if you do it on a video call and pretend the smoke is "part of the ritual." If you're in person, carry a crystal in your pocket—any crystal, doesn't matter—and pull it out to "ground yourself" when the questions get too real. "Hang on, my rose quartz is picking up some chaotic energy. Let me cleanse this convo real quick."

Pro tip: Always have a backup prop. Keep a dog-eared copy of *The Power of Now* on your coffee table, even if you've only read the title. If someone swings by unannounced (rude), gesture vaguely at the book and say, "I'm in a really introspective season right now." They'll nod like they get it, because nobody wants to admit they don't understand Eckhart Tolle. And if all else fails, just mutter something about "shadow work" and watch them back away slowly, terrified of triggering your inner demons.

The Spiritual Lie Starter Pack

To truly master the art of the holy lie, you need the right tools to keep the illusion airtight. Here's your kit for dodging accountability with maximum zen:

- **A Meditation App You Never Use**: Download it, set it to send you push notifications, and screenshot the "You've meditated for 0 minutes this week" popup as proof of your "commitment."

- **A Playlist Called "Vibes Only"**: Fill it with whale sounds and sitar music. Play it loudly when someone calls, then "accidentally" unmute to let them hear your "sacred space."

- **A Fake Guru Name**: If someone presses you for details, say you're following the teachings of "Swami Vibeshifter," a guru you made up who lives in a van in Sedona. Nobody's fact-checking that.

- **A Signature Sigh**: Perfect a deep, soulful sigh that says, "I'm carrying the weight of the cosmos, and you wouldn't understand." Deploy it liberally.

- **Emergency Sage**: Keep a smudge stick in your bag for when you need to stage an impromptu "cleansing" to dodge a conversation. Bonus: It doubles as a great way to scare off nosy coworkers.

When in Doubt, Double Down

The beauty of the "Sorry, I was meditating" lie is its versatility. Forgot your friend's birthday? "I was in a gratitude meditation for you, but it got *so intense* I forgot to text." Blew off a family dinner? "I was visualizing abundance for the whole fam, but my spirit guides kept me in the ether too long." Spilled coffee on your laptop during a work presentation? "I was channeling creative energy, and the universe had other plans." The more absurd the excuse, the more untouchable you become. People don't argue with someone who claims their third eye is on the fritz.

And if someone *really* pushes back—like your mom demanding to know why you haven't called in three weeks—just hit them with the ultimate zen flex: "I've been practicing radical presence, and it's taught me to release attachment to external validation." Then hang up, light some incense, and go back to your dog memes.

You're not lying—you're *living your truth*, and your truth just happens to involve a lot of hummus and zero accountability.

Holy Lies, Holy Life

In the end, "Sorry, I was meditating" isn't just an excuse—it's a lifestyle. It's a sacred pact between you and your couch, a vow to prioritize your vibe over everyone else's drama. Every time you deploy a holy lie, you're not just dodging a phone call or a potluck—you're reclaiming your right to do fckng nothing and do it *gloriously*. So keep your incense lit, your aura polished, and your phone on Do Not Disturb. You're not avoiding life—you're curating nirvana, one dog meme at a time.

Namaste, you lying, vibing legend.

Zen Eighteen

Mindful Ignoring for Beginners (And the Spiritually Advanced)

The path to enlightenment isn't some snooze-fest with lotus flowers and incense—it's a glorious highway of unread messages, each one a cheeky middle finger to the circus of other people's demands. Mindful ignoring isn't about being a jerk; it's a deliberate dodge, a holy art of pruning your mental chaos like a Zen master pruning a bonsai with a chainsaw. You're not dodging folks—you're Marie Kondo-ing your soul's inbox, and Jeff's whiny "k?" in the group chat doesn't spark joy—it sparks a wild urge to yeet your phone into a lavender field and join a Sedona yurt cult with free snacks.

This is the craft of saying "nah" without moving your lips, letting notifications stack up like a tribute to your inner calm. You're not ghosting; you're vibing on a wavelength too cool for Karen's potluck spam. Whether you're a newbie dipping into the zen of zoning out or a spiritually advanced guru who hasn't peeked at voicemail since Y2K, mindful ignoring is your VIP pass to doing f*ckng nothing with the swagger of a Dalai Lama secretly hooked on cat videos.

The Sacred Techniques of Mindful Ignoring

Mindful ignoring is a skill, a vibe, a spiritual mic drop that needs flair and zero apologies. Here's your quirky toolkit to evade, sidestep, and vanish with zen-tastic gusto:

- **The Group Chat Black Hole:** Let that 47-person WhatsApp saga about "Summer BBQ Deets" yell into the void while you sort your sock drawer by vibe (cotton, fuzzy, ethically sourced fuzzy). Extra kudos if you mute it mid-rant about ranch dip being a lifestyle choice.

- **The Soul's Nope Vote:** When "Mom" or "Work" lights up your screen, hear your soul giggle, "Catch you in the next reincarnation!" Send it to voicemail, then smudge your phone with sage to banish its needy vibes.

- **The Slack Zen Chant:** Bury that work Slack thread about "Q3 Synergy Goals" with the holy mantra, *Not my circus, not my Wi-Fi.* If they call you out, claim you were on a "digital detox" (aka marathoning reality TV with nacho grease).

- **The Read Receipt Revolt:** Kill read receipts and let them guess if you're ignoring them or floating on a cloud with no signal. Hint: It's both, and you're loving it.

- **The Delayed Reply Illusion:** If forced to respond, wait 3-5 business days, then hit them with, "I was realigning my chakras; what's the tea?" They'll be too baffled to ping you again.

These aren't just moves—they're ceremonies. Each unread text is a hymn to your peace, each ignored call a love letter to your couch. You're not unreliable—you're a chaos curator, a high priest of "I'll deal when my vibes align."

Handling the Confrontation: The No-Blink Stare

Sooner or later, someone's gonna ambush you with, "Why didn't you reply?" Maybe it's Jeff, waving his "k." like it's a Nobel-worthy epic. Maybe it's your coworker pushing "team bonding yoga" like it's a life-or-death mission. No sweat—you've got the No-Blink Stare, your secret weapon.

Here's the play: Tilt your head like you're channeling a wise ancestor, then drop, "My spirit guide said save my mojo for bigger gigs." Lock eyes. No blinking. Stretch the silence until they're sweating and rethinking their life choices. If they press, sigh like their question's throwing off the universe's groove, and whisper, "I was in a sacred snooze. It's deep." Then sashay off—bonus points if you've got a scarf flapping (even if it's just to grab a soda).

For extra pizzazz, whip out a crystal mid-chat and "purify" the air. Real amethyst? Parking lot pebble? Doesn't matter—wave it like it's zapping their clinginess. On a video call? "Oops" and topple a Himalayan salt lamp for dramatic flair. They'll be too busy searching "sacred snooze" to bug you again.

The Mindful Ignoring Starter Pack

To rule this art, you need gear to keep your ignore game unstoppable. Stock up with:

- **A Phone Case That Shouts "Leave Me Be":** Extra style if it's blinged with "Namaste TF Out" in glitter.

- **A Fake Meditation Timer:** Set it to buzz randomly so you can bolt with, "Gotta meditate—catch you never!"

- **Zen Noise-Canceling Headphones:** Block out the world

with beats or white noise, perfect for pretending you didn't hear Jeff's "k?" rant. Bonus if they're neon and scream, "I'm too cool for you."

- **A Mini Zen Garden:** Keep a tiny sandbox on your desk to rake aimlessly while ignoring emails—watch your coworkers marvel at your "deep focus."

- **Incense Stash:** Light a stick and claim you're in a "cleansing ritual" whenever someone tries to drag you into a meeting. Extra points for funky scents like "Patchouli Panic."

- **Portable Crystal Kit:** Carry a pouch of shiny rocks (real or roadside finds) to whip out during confrontations—perfect for "energy realignment" excuses.

- **Auto-Reply Script:** Set up an email auto-response like, "I'm currently channeling the universe—reply by cosmic decree only," and watch the confusion roll in.

And there you have it—your ultimate guide to mastering mindful ignoring, where every ignored ping is a step toward nirvana, and every unanswered call is a victory lap for your sanity. So go forth, oh enlightened one, and ignore with glee because if the universe can ghost us with Monday mornings, you can totally ghost Jeff's "k?" without a shred of guilt. Now, if you'll excuse me, my spirit guide just texted me about a sale on yurt decor!

Zen Nineteen

GROUP NAPS AS A FORM OF ACTIVISM (VIVA LA REM!)

It's time to rise up... and immediately lie down. Welcome to the revolution that doesn't require you to leave your bed, let alone lace up combat boots: *Naptivism*. In a world that's perpetually on fire—where hustle culture is screaming at you to "grind harder" and your inbox is staging a coup—sometimes the most radical act of defiance is to close your eyes, snore like a chainsaw, and tell productivity to go shove its to-do list where the sun don't shine. And the best part? You don't have to do it alone. Grab your comrades, your coziest blanket, and your finest sleep mask, because group naps are the new sit-ins, and we're here to nap for justice.

Naptivism isn't just a snooze; it's a movement, a middle finger to the capitalist hamster wheel, a collective yawn in the face of brunch fatigue and Zoom burnout. Picture it: a field of rebels in matching flannel pajamas, sprawled out on yoga mats, armed with lavender eye pillows and a shared Spotify playlist called "Snooze Anarchy." This is civil disobedience, but comfier. It's protest with a side of snacks. It's a revolution that smells like chamomile and dreams of a world where "adulting" means mandatory nap breaks and government-issued weighted blankets. Down with the grind. Up with your feet. *Viva la REM!*

The Naptivist's Manifesto

Naptivism isn't about laziness; it's about *intention*. You're not just napping; you're dismantling the patriarchy one drool stain at a time. You're rejecting the toxic myth that you're only valuable when you're awake and caffeinated. Here's how to organize your own group nap, the most radical act of doing f*ckng nothing since you "forgot" to RSVP to Karen's vision board party:

1. **Assemble Your Nap Posse**: Round up your fellow revolutionaries. Those ride-or-die friends who get that "self-care" means eating Goldfish crackers in bed. Everyone brings something: a sleeping bag, a snack pouch (Cheetos are the official sponsor of Naptivism), a lavender diffuser, or a playlist of whale sounds so soothing it could sedate a toddler mid-tantrum.

2. **Set the Scene**: Find a sacred napping ground: a park, a living room, or that one friend's basement that smells vaguely of patchouli and regret. Lay out blankets, fluff pillows, and banish anything that screams "productivity," like laptops or that guy who keeps talking about his "side hustle."

3. **Chant Your Demands**: As you drift into the sweet embrace of REM, chant softly to rally the troops:

    - "What do we want? REST! When do we want it? RIGHT AFTER THIS COOKI—zzzzz."

    - "No grind! No stress! Give us naps or give us... *yawn*...

whatever!"

"Eight hours of sleep! Eight hours of sleep! Plus a snack break, because we're not monsters!"

4. **Nap with Purpose**: This isn't just a power nap—it's a *power statement*. Visualize a world where meetings are replaced with siestas, where "hustle" is a dirty word, and where adult pacifiers are covered by insurance. Dream big, then drool bigger.

When you wake, foggy-eyed and slightly disoriented, you'll feel the rush of revolution in your veins (or maybe that's just low blood sugar from all the Cheetos). You've just napped for a cause, you glorious, sleep-deprived warrior.

The Naptivism Starter Pack

To pull off a group nap that shakes the system to its core, you need the right gear. Here's your activist arsenal for maximum snooze impact:

- **A Protest Pillow**: Preferably one that says "Nap Now, Adult Later" in glittery embroidery. Bonus points if it's so fluffy it could double as a flotation device.

- **A Sleep Mask with Attitude**: Get one that says "Do Not Disturb Unless You're Bringing Tacos." It's both a fashion statement and a boundary.

- **A Snack Stash**: Pack enough Goldfish, granola bars, and emergency chocolate to fuel a nap marathon. Pro tip: Crumbs are the glitter of Naptivism—sprinkle liberally.

- **A Portable Diffuser**: Blast lavender or eucalyptus to create a "no hustle zone." If anyone tries to talk about work, aim the mist at them like a spiritual squirt gun.

- **A Manifesto Zine**: Print out a tiny pamphlet titled "The Nap Agenda" with slogans like "Snooze to Subvert" and "Burnout Is Cancelled." Hand it out to confused passersby for maximum chaos.

Handling the Haters

Not everyone will understand your radical commitment to napping. Some capitalist shill—probably named Chad—will roll up with his protein shake and his "early bird gets the worm" nonsense, demanding to know why you're "wasting the day." Hit them with a serene smile and say, "I'm dismantling systemic burnout one nap at a time. Care to join the revolution?" Then hand them a pillow and watch them short-circuit.

If your boss catches wind of your Naptivist activities, don't panic. Just tell them you're "recharging your creative energy to optimize workplace synergy." Sprinkle in some buzzwords like "mindful recalibration" or "holistic productivity reset," and they'll be too confused to fire you. And if your mom calls to ask why you're napping in a park instead of "living your potential," sigh deeply and say, "I'm manifesting abundance through rest, Mom. It's quantum." Then hang up and roll over for round two.

The Dream of a Better World

Every group nap is a protest against a world that glorifies exhaustion. It's a middle finger to the 5 a.m. hustle, the 9-to-5 grind, and the expectation that you should "seize the day" when you'd rather seize a pillow. When you wake from your Naptivist slumber, crusty-eyed and defiant, you'll have dreamt of a utopia where nap pods replace cubicles, where "self-care" means a federally mandated siesta, and where weighted blankets are tax-deductible.

This is the future Naptivism fights for: a world where "I'm tired" is a valid excuse to cancel everything, where adult pacifiers come in fun colors, and where nobody ever asks you to brunch because they're too busy napping. So gather your comrades, fluff your pillows, and nap like the revolution depends on it—because it does. Down with burnout. Up with your feet. *Viva la REM, you sleepy, rebellious legends!*

Zen Twenty

Dating While Spiritually Unavailable (Swipe Left on Emotional Labor)

You're not single—you're in a passionate, soul-binding love affair with your own nervous system, and baby, it's *exclusive*. You've got a velvet-roped VIP pass to your inner peace, and you're not about to let some dude with a Bumble profile, a man bun, and a bio that says "just here for the vibes" gatecrash your aura's private party. Dating? Please. That's a dystopian Hunger Games of emotional labor, and you've already burned your invitation, saged the ashes, and scattered them in a full-moon ritual. You're not just benched; you've catapulted yourself into the spiritual nosebleeds, sipping overpriced kombucha, vibing with your fiddle-leaf fig, and whispering affirmations to your Roomba like it's your life coach.

You've evolved. You've grown. You've ugly-cried into a $16 gluten-free scone while rage-journaling about your mom's passive-aggressive texts ("Hope you're doing OKAY, sweetie; call me when you're less BUSY"). You've done the *work*, staring into the abyss of your childhood trauma until it blinked first, leaving you with a vision board covered in glitter glue and a sage stick so big it could double as a melee weapon. But dating? That's like signing up for a CrossFit class taught by your ex's new partner, who definitely Venmo-requested you $3.47 for "shared coffee" in 2022. Hard pass. You're too busy curating your chakra playlist to deal with that noise.

Your Dating Profile Would Be a Glorious Dumpster Fire

If you were forced at crystal-point to join a dating app, your profile would be a neon-flashing shrine to spiritual unavailability, so chaotic it'd make even the most enlightened yogi swipe left in fear. Picture this masterpiece:

- **Bio**: "Seeking someone who respects that I'll ghost for a week to recalibrate my chakras and return with a new aura color (currently rocking a chaotic chartreuse). No Chads, no 'wyd' texts, no vibes below 432 Hz."

- **Prompts**: "Must love 23-minute eye contact marathons, absolute silence, and zero expectations. Bonus points if you can spot the difference between my Mercury retrograde breakdowns and my 'I ate too much hummus' breakdowns."

- **Ideal Date**: "A sound bath followed by 72 hours of not speaking, not texting, and not existing in the same dimension. Just pure vibes, no pets, no kids, no eye contact unless it's with my oracle deck."

- **Dealbreaker**: "If you text 'wyd?' I'll assume you're a CIA operative sent to sabotage my vibrational alignment. Also, if your bio says 'tacos are life,' I'm reporting you to the universe for lack of originality."

You swipe through profiles like a monk skimming ancient scrolls, but instead of wisdom, you're dodging guys named Brad who list "craft beer" as a core value and women who post gym selfies with captions like "Chasing endorphins and sunsets." You spot a cute profile—someone holding a puppy, quoting Rumi, looking like they might get your vibe. For a reckless half-second, you consider messaging. Then they text, "wyd?" and your soul astral-projects to a dimension where phones don't exist. You consider replying, "Oh, just syncing my root chakra with this $400 weighted blanket and a bag of Flamin' Hot Cheetos," but instead, you yeet your phone into a pile of ethically sourced amethysts and swan-dive into an herbal bath like a lavender-scented phoenix rising from the ashes of bad vibes. *Reborn, unbothered, and untouchable.*

Your Heart's on a Time-Out (and It's Fully Booked)

Let's be real: your heart isn't ready for prime time. You just got it back from your last therapist, and it's still in the shop getting its aura buffed, its edges reinforced with energetic duct tape. It's cocooned in metaphysical bubble wrap, guarded by a vision board that screams "BOUNDARIES" in glitter gel pen and a dream journal that's basically just 47 pages of "Why am I like this?" You're not saying you'll *never* date again, but your nervous system is the bouncer at Club You, and it's got a strict guest list: nobody gets in without a divine sign, like a prophetic squirrel handing you a fortune cookie that says, "Chill, fam, you're thriving solo."

Even if the universe sent you a neon-flashing "GO DATE" signal, the logistics are a nightmare. A date? In *this* economy? You'd have to schedule it between your meditation app's passive-aggressive reminders ("You haven't meditated in 17 days, are you okay?"), your biweekly existential meltdowns, and that sacred monthly ritual where you rearrange your essential oils by emotional resonance (bergamot for joy, patchouli for "leave me alone"). And what do you even wear? Your wardrobe is 85% linen caftans, 10% sweatpants you've gaslit yourself into calling "athleisure," and 5% that one thrift-store kimono you bought because it "felt like your soul's true form." Showing up to a date in a caftan says, "I'm here to cleanse your aura or curse your bloodline, your choice," and nobody's ready for that energy at a wine bar.

The Date That Never Happened (Thank the Cosmos)

Imagine you actually say yes to a date because apparently you hate yourself. You're at some overpriced café, trying to explain why you brought your own reusable straw, a vial of moon-charged water, and a tiny quartz crystal "for grounding." Your date asks, "So, what do you do for fun?" and your brain blue-screens. Fun? You haven't had "fun" since you accidentally cackled during a silent meditation retreat and got death-stared by a room full of kombucha-drinking yogis. You mumble something about "curating my inner peace," and they nod like they get it, but you can see them mentally Googling "how to flee a date with a crystal-obsessed gremlin."

Then comes the killer question: "What are you looking for?" Oh, honey. You're looking for someone who can handle your 4 a.m. panic attacks about whether reality is a simulation, who won't bat an eye when you cancel plans because "Venus is in Scorpio and the vibes are *off*," and who gets that your love language is Post-it notes with affirmations like "You're enough, but please don't text me for 48 hours." You don't need a partner; you need a *vibe sommelier*, someone who can pair your existential dread with the perfect guided meditation. Good luck finding *that* on Tinder.

And don't even get you started on the small talk. They ask about your hobbies, and you accidentally let slip that you spent last weekend arguing with your Roomba because it got stuck under the couch during a "spiritual decluttering." They mention their dog, and you counter with, "That's cool, but my Himalayan salt lamp, Gerald, has been teaching me about boundaries." By the time they ask about your job, you're halfway through a monologue about how you're "manifesting abundance" by avoiding all emails marked "urgent." They're already plotting their escape, and you're plotting your next nap.

Namastay Single, You Glorious Disaster

In the end, you're not just single; you're *Zen single*, a radiant, unavailable deity married to your own vibe in a ceremony officiated by your therapist and a $200 Himalayan salt lamp named Gerald. You've got your rituals: the sage smudging, the unhinged poetry in your journal about the divine feminine, the 3 a.m. tarot pulls that always say "focus on yourself" (rude, but fair). You don't need a plus-one when your plus-one is a $75 scented candle that smells like "inner peace and petty revenge."

So keep swiping left on emotional labor, blocking "wyd?" texts like they're psychic attacks, and doing fckng nothing with the flair of a spiritual rockstar. You're not avoiding love; you're curating nirvana, one caftan at a time. Namaste, single, you radiant, unavailable legend.

Zen Twenty-One

YOU ARE ENOUGH, EVEN IF YOU DID NOTHING TODAY

Let's cut the crap: productivity is a cult, and you, my friend, are staging a one-person sit-in against it. Today? You didn't light a single candle, unless you count accidentally setting fire to your napkin while trying to microwave a burrito. You didn't answer emails; your inbox is basically a digital landfill at this point. Your Fitbit thinks you've flatlined because you've spent eight hours rotating between bed, fridge, and vague existential scrolling on your phone, pondering if cats know they're cute or if they're just naturally smug. And guess what? You still exist. You still matter. You're still enough—pajama-clad, unwashed, and gloriously unproductive.

This chapter is your spiritual permission slip to absolutely flop. You didn't self-actualize today? Neither did Buddha every Tuesday—those enlightenment breaks were real, people. Let your to-do list weep in the corner like a needy ex who keeps texting "u up?" while you wrap yourself in a blanket burrito and whisper to the universe, "I *am* the task." You're not just doing nothing—you're mastering the ancient art of *being*, and that's a flex worth celebrating.

The Productivity Cult: A Ridiculous Conspiracy

Picture this: it's 3 PM, and you're still in your pajamas, which, let's be honest, are just glorified sweatpants with a questionable salsa stain. Your to-do list is glaring at you from the kitchen counter like that one relative who always asks for money, but you've chosen to ignore it. Good for you. We've all been brainwashed by the Cult of Productivity, a shadowy organization that insists if you're not crossing off tasks like a caffeinated robot, you're failing at life. They've got us believing that every minute must be *optimized*, every day a checklist of triumphs. But here's the dirty little secret: even the most productive people—those Type-A freaks who meal-prep on Sundays and color-code their sock drawers—have days where they just *can't*. And that's not a flaw; it's a feature.

Productivity is like a needy pet that keeps pawing at you for attention. "Feed me! Walk me! Give me purpose!" it whines, while you're over here trying to figure out if it's socially acceptable to eat cereal for dinner again. Spoiler: it is. The cult wants you to think your worth is tied to how many emails you send or how many steps your Fitbit logs, but let's get real—your Fitbit doesn't even know you're a person. It's just a tiny judgmental wrist cop, and today, it's filing a missing persons report because you've been horizontal since noon. Screw that noise. You're not a machine, and you don't need to be "on" 24/7. Sometimes, the most radical act of rebellion is to say, "Nah," and let yourself be a human slug for a day. Slime on, you majestic creature.

The Zen of Doing Jack Squat

Now, let's get spiritual about this. In Zen, there's this beautiful concept of "just being"—existing in the moment without the need to *do* anything. So when you're sprawled on the couch, staring at the ceiling fan like it's a hypnotic portal to another dimension, you're not being lazy—you're practicing advanced Zen techniques. Congrats, you're basically a monk now. The Buddha didn't sit under that Bodhi tree because he had a deadline; he sat there because he was tired, and enlightenment was just a happy bonus. You're in good company, my friend.

Philosophers have been onto this for centuries. Take Lao Tzu, who said, "By doing nothing, everything is done." Sure, he probably meant something profound about the flow of the universe, but I choose to interpret it as permission to binge-watch reality TV while eating chips straight from the bag. Or how about Socrates? "I know that I know nothing," he mused, which is basically the vibe when you've spent an hour googling "Why do I feel guilty for not doing anything?" instead of, you know, doing anything. These wise folks knew the score: existence isn't about constant output. It's about showing up, even if "showing up" means napping through your alarm and calling it "meditation."

Here's the kicker: you did *plenty* today without even trying. Check out these unsung victories:

- **Blinked approximately 14,400 times.** That's Olympic-level eyelid endurance.

- **Converted oxygen into carbon dioxide like a pro.** Plants everywhere are thanking you.

- **Kept your body temperature at 98.6 degrees.** Homeostasis? Nailed it.

- **Thought about doing laundry but didn't.** Strategic energy conservation. Future you will appreciate the effort (or lack thereof).

You're a walking, breathing miracle, and you didn't even need to leave the house. Take that, productivity cult.

Embracing the Holy Art of Nothingness

But let's talk about the elephant in the room: guilt. That little voice in your head that whispers, "You're not doing enough," like a passive-aggressive life coach. Here's how to deal with it: when guilt knocks, let it in, offer it a cup of tea, and then kindly ask it to leave because you're busy doing nothing. Whisper back, "I'm exactly where I need to be right now," and watch it sulk away. Guilt is just a feeling, not a fact. You don't have to RSVP to its pity party.

Need some practical tips for embracing your inner sloth? Try these:

- **Turn your to-do list into a ta-da list.** Write down everything you *didn't* do and celebrate it. "Didn't pay bills—kept the suspense alive!" "Didn't exercise—gave my couch some quality time!" Instant gratification.

- **Rename your laziness.** Call it "intentional stillness" or "cosmic recharging." Sounds way sexier than "procrastination," doesn't it?

- **Befriend your mess.** That pile of dishes? It's a monument to your humanity. That unmade bed? A canvas of dreams. You're an artist, not a slob.

And if someone dares ask what you did today, just smile mysteriously and say, "I was busy being." They'll either think you're profound or unhinged, but either way, you win. You're not just existing—you're thriving in the sacred space between effort and ease, a sage in sweatpants, a poet of the pause.

You're a Legend, Full Stop

So here's the gospel truth: you breathed today, didn't you? You hydrated (maybe accidentally, via that half-empty soda can you found under the couch)? You survived another spin around the sun in this cosmic joke of a simulation. That's enough. That's *everything*. You don't need to prove your worth to anyone—not your boss, not your Fitbit, not even that nagging voice that sounds suspiciously like your high school gym teacher.

You're a masterpiece of non-doing, a living koan in a world obsessed with answers. The next time someone asks what you accomplished today, just wink and say, "I perfected the art of existence." Then retreat to your blanket fort, where you reign supreme as the high priestess—or priest—of chill. Namaste, you glorious, unproductive icon. You're not just enough; you're a legend in sweatpants, and the universe is lucky to have you, salsa stains and all.

Zen Twenty-Two
The Tao of Takeout

Ordering Pad Thai in Pajamas: A Monk's Guide to Modern Enlightenment

There are ancient scrolls—buried in some forgotten cave, probably next to a half-eaten spring roll—that detail the sacred ritual of ordering pad Thai while refusing to put on real pants. You, dear reader, are the modern monk honoring that tradition, a sage in sweatpants, a prophet of procrastination. The Tao of Takeout isn't just a way of eating; it's a way of *being*—a path to enlightenment so chill it could make a Himalayan guru jealous. Forget fasting in a monastery or chanting at dawn; your spiritual journey begins with a phone, a couch, and a willingness to embrace the divine chaos of food delivered by strangers.

The Tao of Takeout teaches us three eternal truths:

- **All cravings are valid.** Whether it's 2 a.m. dumplings or a questionable burrito, your hunger is a sacred whisper from the universe. Ignore it at your peril.

- **Cooking is optional if you have a phone and low standards.** Why wrestle with a stove when the cosmos has blessed you with apps and a credit card? The stove is for suckers.

- **Food prepared by strangers tastes better when consumed horizontal.** Science can't explain it, but the couch-to-mouth pipeline is a direct route to nirvana.

The Tao doesn't judge your Uber Eats history, even if it's 90% late-night mozzarella sticks and regret. The Tao understands that enlightenment is sometimes deep-fried, arrives in a crinkly paper bag, and comes with extra soy sauce packets you'll never use. So bow to the delivery driver like they're a sage bearing sacred scrolls (because they are), tip with the reverence of a pilgrim, and recycle those chopsticks into altar incense. Dinner is served, and so is your soul. Namaste, you greasy-fingered legend.

The Sacred Selection: Choosing Your Meal Like a Zen Master

The journey begins with the Selection Ceremony, a meditative process so profound it could rival a monk's morning chants. Open your app of choice: Uber Eats, DoorDash, or that one sketchy site that still takes cash—and let the endless scroll of restaurants wash over you like a digital river of possibility. This is not mere browsing; this is *contemplation*. Each restaurant name is a mantra, each menu a sacred text. Does the whisper of "Dragon Wok" stir your soul, or is it the siren call of "Pizza Paradise" that beckons your inner hunger? Close your eyes (but not really, because you need to see the screen), breathe deeply, and let your gut guide you. It's not indigestion; it's intuition.

As you peruse the options, remember: the Tao of Takeout embraces all cuisines equally. Sushi is as holy as sliders, and tacos are just burritos that haven't found their true form yet. If you're feeling indecisive, consult the oracle of online reviews, where enlightened beings (and that one guy who's mad about extra napkins) leave cryptic clues about portion sizes and spice levels. A five-star rating is a blessing; a one-star rant is a lesson in detachment. Choose wisely, but not too wisely—perfection is the enemy of a full stomach.

The Waiting Meditation: Patience, Pillows, and Pre-Feast Prep

Once you've placed your order, you enter the sacred phase of Waiting Meditation. This is not idle time; it's a masterclass in patience, a chance to practice the ancient art of *doing absolutely nothing* while your food hurtles toward you at the speed of a hungover delivery driver. The Tao teaches that anticipation is half the meal, so use this time to align your chakras—or, more practically, to align your couch cushions for optimal lounging. A well-placed pillow can be as enlightening as a well-timed fortune cookie, and your spine will thank you later.

If the wait feels eternal, resist the urge to refresh the tracking screen every 30 seconds like a caffeinated squirrel. Instead, engage in mindful activities: stare at the ceiling and ponder the meaning of life, or debate whether your cat's judgmental gaze means it wants your pad Thai. You could also use this time to sage your living room, but let's be real—you're not doing that. The Tao of Takeout embraces the chaos of unlit candles and unvacuumed floors. Your vibe is already set to "I'm not leaving this couch," and that's a spiritual stance worth respecting.

The Arrival: A Feast for the Senses (and the Sweatpants)

Then, the moment arrives. A knock at the door—or a notification ping, because who answers doors anymore?—signals the end of your meditation and the start of your feast. Behold, the delivery driver: a modern-day bodhisattva, a sage in a hoodie, bearing gifts of grease and glory. Tip them not just with money but with a nod so reverent it could be mistaken for a bow. They are the unsung heroes of your enlightenment, the ferrymen of your food journey, and they deserve your deepest respect (and maybe an extra dollar for braving your apartment's sketchy stairs).

As you unwrap the bounty, let the crinkle of the bag be your Zen bell, calling you into the present moment. Inhale the steam like it's incense, and arrange your spread with the care of a monk setting an altar. There's no wrong way to do this—whether you're a "separate containers" purist or a "dump it all on one plate" anarchist, the Tao embraces your method. Then, assume your position: horizontal, vertical, or somewhere in between, as long as you're comfortable and your pants are elastic.

The Consumption: A Bite-by-Bite Path to Nirvana

Now, the sacred act of eating. Let each bite be a mantra, each flavor a step closer to the divine. Chew slowly, not because you're savoring the food (though you are), but because you're too lazy to get up for a napkin. The Tao of Takeout doesn't discriminate between spring rolls and sushi rolls, between sweet and sour, between "this is definitely not what I ordered" and "this is exactly what I needed." All is equal in the great buffet of life, and every mouthful is a reminder that you are here, you are hungry, and you are *thriving*.

If you're dining solo, let the silence be your companion—or, more likely, let the dulcet tones of *Love Island* reruns be your soundtrack. If you're sharing with others, practice the ancient art of "don't touch my fries," a boundary-setting exercise as old as time. And remember: the Tao teaches that fortune cookies are not just desserts; they are prophecies. Crack one open, read your fate, and then eat the evidence. If it says, "You will find peace in unexpected places," nod sagely and think, "Yeah, like the bottom of this lo mein container."

The Aftermath: Embracing the Cycle of Consumption and Clutter

Post-feast, as you survey the wreckage of wrappers, sauce packets, and that one chopstick that somehow ended up under the couch, feel no shame. The Tao of Takeout embraces the full cycle of consumption and clutter—your living room is now a shrine to your satisfaction, a monument to your ability to do absolutely nothing and still feel like a king. If guilt creeps in about the mess, banish it with a single thought: "I am one with the chaos, and the chaos is one with me."

When it's time to clean up (or not), do so with intention. Recycle the containers like you're saving the planet one greasy box at a time, and stash those extra soy sauce packets in your drawer of infinite possibilities. You never know when you'll need to bless a bland meal with the gift of sodium. And if you find a stray noodle under your coffee table three days later, don't fret—it's just the universe reminding you that joy lingers, even in the form of forgotten carbs.

The Tao of Takeout: A Conclusion Worth Digesting

In the end, the Tao of Takeout is not just about food—it's about *freedom*. Freedom from the tyranny of cooking, from the expectation of "real" pants, from the idea that you need to do anything more than exist and enjoy. You didn't just order dinner; you participated in a sacred ritual of self-care, a middle finger to productivity, a love letter to your own laziness. So the next time someone asks what you're doing for dinner, smile like a sage, gesture to your phone, and say, "I'm consulting the ancient scrolls." Then order that pad Thai, sprawl on your couch, and let the universe handle the rest. Namaste, you enlightened, take-out-ordering legend.

Zen Twenty-Three

Letting Go of Ambition Without Crying (Much)

Remember when you were going to be a world-famous author, open a vegan dog café, or invent a biodegradable iPhone that composts itself after every iOS update? Yeah, so does your inner overachiever, who's currently ugly-crying into a pint of Ben & Jerry's while binge-watching *The Great British Baking Show* for the third time this month. Back then, you had dreams so big they needed their own zip code—dreams of TED Talks, book tours, and maybe even a Nobel Prize for inventing a sock that never gets lost in the dryer. But now? Now, you just want to stare at a wall for three hours without anyone asking if you're okay. Maybe eat a croissant. Possibly take a nap. And honestly, babe, that's growth.

Letting go of ambition isn't failure—it's *liberation*. It's realizing that climbing the ladder is exhausting, and maybe you'd rather sit at the bottom, eat a croissant, and contemplate the meaning of life. Or, you know, just eat the croissant and call it a day. Both are valid, and both are better than pretending you still care about "crushing it" when your biggest goal is remembering where you left your keys.

The Ambition Graveyard: Where Dreams Go to Die (and That's Okay)

We all had dreams. Big, ridiculous dreams. Like becoming a professional unicorn wrangler or inventing a self-cleaning sock that pairs itself. Maybe you were going to launch a startup that turns your face into a potato for Zoom calls (wait, that's already a thing?) or write a memoir so raw it'd make Brené Brown blush. But let's be real: the world doesn't need another app, another TED Talk, or another "disruptive" idea that's just a juicer but for socks. What the world needs is people who are okay with not being okay all the time—people who can laugh at their own absurdity and find joy in the mundane.

Your ambition graveyard is full of half-baked ideas and abandoned passion projects, and that's not a tragedy—it's a *triumph*. It means you've lived, you've tried, and now you're wise enough to know that "success" is just a fancy word for "someone else's checklist." So pour one out for your inner hustler, who's probably still sobbing over that vision board you made in 2017. Then, let it go. You're not here to change the world—you're here to *be* in it, and that's a hell of a lot harder than it sounds.

The Joy of Mundanity: Finding Nirvana in Doing Nothing

Here's the tea: ambition is overrated, and mundanity is where the magic happens. You could still change the world, sure—*or* you could organize your spice drawer alphabetically and feel like a goddamn deity. Imagine the rush of power when you realize your cumin is finally next to your coriander. That's not just organization; that's *enlightenment*. You're not just a person with a tidy kitchen—you're a sage of the spice rack, a prophet of paprika.

And let's talk about the small wins, because they're the real MVPs. Did you make your bed today? No? Perfect; you've embraced the chaos. Did you accidentally wear your shirt inside out and decide to own it? That's not a mistake; that's *avant-garde fashion*. Did you spend an hour scrolling through TikTok videos of dogs in sweaters? You weren't procrastinating—you were *studying joy*. The point is, life's not about the big, shiny achievements; it's about the tiny, ridiculous moments that make you snort-laugh at your own existence.

The Tears Will Come (But So Will the Snacks)

Let's be real: letting go of ambition isn't all rainbows and unbothered vibes. There will be tears. You'll mourn your hustle like it's an ex who still owes you money. You'll stare at your old vision board—covered in glitter glue and unrealistic expectations—and wonder where it all went wrong. But then, mid-sob, you'll catch a glimpse of your houseplant (the one you've somehow kept alive despite your best efforts), and you'll think, *This is enough. I am enough. Also, I'm out of cinnamon, and that's a problem.*

That's when you'll realize peace isn't found at the top of the mountain; it's found in the snack drawer, in the quiet moments when you're not trying to be anything but yourself. So grab that croissant, flop onto your couch, and let the world spin on without you. You're not just enough—you're a legend in sweatpants, a sage of simplicity, a goddamn poet of the pause. And if anyone asks what you're doing with your life, just smile and say, "I'm busy being," then retreat to your spice drawer to bask in your own mundane glory. Namaste, you beautifully unambitious icon.

Zen Twenty-Four

ENLIGHTENMENT IS PROBABLY JUST LOW BLOOD SUGAR

You're not having a spiritual awakening—you're just *hangry*. That "oneness with the void" feeling? That's your stomach digesting air like a sad, empty balloon. Those goosebumps of clarity? Nope, that's malnutrition doing a TED Talk on your soul. And let's be real: the only "higher plane" you're tapping into is the one where you forgot to eat breakfast and now think you're communing with the universe. Spoiler: the universe is just your body screaming, "FEED ME, YOU CHAOTIC GREMLIN!"

But here's the kicker—*let's normalize snack-based enlightenment*. Because the greatest truths don't come from fasting in a cave or chanting at dawn; they hit right after a graham cracker, somewhere between "I am one with all things" and "Oh god, I need a nap." Many prophets probably just needed a sandwich and a juice box before they started scribbling down revelations. Moses? Wandering the desert for 40 years? Dude was probably just looking for a decent falafel stand.

Picture this: You're sitting cross-legged on your yoga mat, eyes closed, trying to channel your inner guru. Suddenly, you feel a wave of emptiness wash over you. "Is this it?" you wonder. "Am I finally connecting with the cosmos?" Then, your stomach growls so loudly it could wake a pharaoh from a 3,000-year nap. Nope, not enlightenment—just your body begging for a burrito. The only "transcendence" here is transcending your last meal into a distant memory.

The Snack Path to Nirvana: A Beginner's Guide

Forget silent retreats and overpriced wellness seminars—your spiritual journey starts in the pantry. Here's how to tell if you're enlightened or just starving:

- **The "I'm One with the Universe" Vibe**: You're meditating, feeling a deep, cosmic connection. Then your stomach lets out a roar that could soundtrack a Godzilla flick. Plot twist: you're not ascending—you're just digesting nothing.

- **The "Everyone Is Toxic" Epiphany**: You're *this close* to texting your entire contact list, "You're all energy vampires!" Then you eat a handful of almonds, and suddenly, Karen's potluck invite seems… tolerable. Crisis averted.

- **The "I Need to Move to a Desert" Urge**: You're packing a bag, ready to renounce society and live off-grid. But wait—did you skip lunch? A protein shake later, and suddenly, your couch looks way comfier than a sand dune.

The Hangry Prophet's Playbook

When the line between "awakening" and "I need a taco" gets blurry, follow these pro tips to keep your soul (and stomach) in check:

- **Before you journal about your higher self, eat something.** Trust me, your profound thoughts will sound a lot less like "I am one with the cosmos" and more like "I am one with this PB&J" once you've had a bite. Otherwise, your journal's just a hunger-fueled rant about how the void smells like regret.

- **Before you renounce all your relationships, have a granola bar.** That "everyone is toxic" vibe might just be your blood sugar talking. A handful of trail mix could save your friendships—and stop you from sending that dramatic "I'm done with humanity" group text.

- **Before you move to the desert to find God, check if you've skipped lunch.** The desert's hot, God's probably busy, and you're not Moses (see falafel theory above). A protein shake might be the miracle you're chasing—no sand required.

Snack Hacks for the Spiritually Confused

Still unsure if it's nirvana or low blood sugar? These divine snacks will guide you back to reality:

- **The Graham Cracker Guru**: One bite, and you're back from the brink. Enlightenment tastes like cinnamon and a vague sense of "I'll figure it out later."

- **The Holy Handful of Trail Mix**: Nuts for clarity, raisins for wisdom, and M&Ms because who said enlightenment can't be fun?

- **The Divine PB&J**: A sandwich so sacred, it could broker peace treaties. Cut it diagonally for extra zen points—symmetry is spiritual, right?

If all else fails, toast is your spirit guide. Slap some butter on it, whisper "I am enough," and call it a day. You're not broken—you're just hangry. Eat something divine, like a Pop-Tart with existential sprinkles, and watch the universe make sense again.

The Crumb-Covered Conclusion

So next time you feel like you're on the brink of a spiritual breakthrough, pause and ask yourself, "When did I last eat?" If the answer is "sometime last Tuesday," grab a snack before you start packing for that ashram. The path to enlightenment is paved with crumbs, and the universe speaks to us through our stomachs. You're not failing at life—you're just under-snacked. So grab some nachos, salute your inner hangry prophet, and namaste your way to the fridge. Snack now, ascend later.

Zen Twenty-Five

WHEN IN DOUBT, BECOME ONE WITH THE BLANKET

The Sacred Swaddle: Your Guide to Ghosting Reality in Style

The world's too loud—screaming notifications, honking cars, that one coworker who won't stop humming "Happy Birthday" three weeks after the party. Your brain's buffering like a 90s dial-up modem, and those breathing exercises you tried? They felt like homework assigned by a yoga influencer with too many teeth. It's time to ditch the chaos and embrace the ultimate act of surrender: wrap yourself in the blanket. Merge. *Become* it. There is no you. There is only warm. Only soft. Only the sweet, sweet stillness of a human burrito saying "nope" to existence. Welcome to the sacred art of blanket practice, where doing f*ckng nothing is not just a choice; it's a *lifestyle*.

Blanket practice isn't just about hiding from your to-do list (though it's great for that); it's a spiritual rebellion, a middle finger to the grind, a cozy cocoon where you can ghost capitalism and still look like a Pinterest board come to life. You're not lazy—you're a boundary-setting deity, a swaddled sage, a burrito of "don't even ask me about my day." So pile on the fleece, fluff the pillows, and let the world spin without you. You're too busy being one with the blanket, and that's the most enlightened flex there is.

The Holy Trinity of Blanket Practice

Blanket practice teaches us three eternal truths, whispered in the soft folds of your favorite throw:

- **Silence is powerful.** No need to answer emails, texts, or your neighbor's knock about "just borrowing some sugar." The blanket muffles all, like a noise-canceling headphone for your soul.

- **Hibernation is holy.** Bears don't apologize for napping through winter, and neither should you. Your blanket cocoon is a sacred retreat, a vibe temple where time doesn't exist.

- **You can ghost capitalism and still be stylish.** Who needs a power suit when you've got a quilted cape that says, "I'm not leaving this couch, but I look fabulous doing it"?

These truths aren't just philosophies—they're your new life mottos. Write them on a Post-it, stick it to your fridge, then ignore it because you're too busy merging with your blanket like a zen caterpillar dreaming of snacks.

The Blanket Burrito Ritual: Your Step-by-Step Guide to Nope

Becoming one with the blanket isn't just a vibe; it's a *ritual*, a sacred sequence that transforms you from "overwhelmed human" to "untouchable fluff deity." Here's how to do it with maximum zen and minimum effort:

1. **Choose Your Blanket**: Select a blanket that speaks to

your soul—fuzzy fleece, weighted wonder, or that ratty afghan your grandma knit that smells like nostalgia and mothballs. No blanket? Pile on hoodies, towels, or that one bathrobe you stole from a hotel. The Tao of Blanket accepts all fabrics.

2. **Assume the Position**: Flop onto your couch, bed, or floor—anywhere gravity's your friend. Wrap yourself tightly, leaving just enough room for your face (breathing is nice) and one hand (for snacks). You're not a person anymore—you're a burrito of boundaries.

3. **Enter the Void**: Close your eyes, or stare at the ceiling like it's spilling cosmic secrets. Let thoughts drift—bills, deadlines, that weird noise your fridge makes—like clouds in a sky you don't have to deal with. You're too swaddled for stress.

4. **Ghost the World**: Silence your phone, or better yet, yeet it into a pile of laundry. If someone knocks, pretend you're a sentient quilt who doesn't speak English. Your only obligation is to stay cozy.

5. **Optional Snack Integration**: Stash Goldfish, a rogue Twix, or that half-eaten granola bar you found under the couch. Nibble with intention, like you're communing with the divine (because you are).

The Blanket Burrito Starter Pack

To master this practice, you need gear that screams, "I'm unavailable but thriving." Here's your toolkit:

- **A Blanket Fort-Worthy Throw**: Bonus points if it's got a stain named Greg or smells like "cozy chaos."

- **Snacks Within Arm's Reach**: Pretzels, M&Ms, or a bag of chips so stale they're practically relics. Crumbs are your glitter.

- **A Vague Stare**: Look like you're pondering existence when you're really wondering if your cat's plotting a coup.

- **A "Do Not Disturb" Vibe**: No props needed—your swaddled silence says, "Talk to the blanket, I'm out."

Deflecting the Blanket Haters

The world's full of productivity cops who'll try to drag you out of your cocoon. Your roommate storms in, "Are you still on the couch?" Channel your inner sloth sage and mumble, "I'm in a sacred swaddle, Karen. Respect the process." Your mom calls, "Why aren't you doing something?" Hit her with, "I'm doing the most important thing—existing. It's quantum, Mom, look it up." And if some hustle bro in a $200 tracksuit tells you to "seize the day," smirk through your blanket folds and whisper, "I'm seizing this nap, Chad. Catch up."

For extra flair, keep a notebook nearby with one word scribbled in glitter pen: "Serenity." When questioned, point to it dramatically and say, "This is my mantra." They'll back off, terrified of your unhinged energy, leaving you free to burrito in peace.

The Philosophy of Fluff: Why Blanket Practice Is Peak Zen

Let's get deep for a sec. Zen is all about presence, about being exactly where you are without judgment. And where are you? Wrapped in a blanket, ignoring your inbox, vibing like a sage who's traded lotus poses for Netflix. That's not laziness—that's *enlightenment*. The Dalai Lama probably has a secret blanket fort where he hides from his calendar, and Lao Tzu's "do nothing, and all is done" was clearly written mid-nap under a quilt. You're in elite company, my friend.

The blanket is more than fabric; it's a metaphor for self-acceptance. It doesn't care if you haven't showered since Tuesday or if your to-do list is longer than a CVS receipt. It just holds you, like the universe would if it had arms and a polyester blend. Every time you swaddle yourself, you're saying, "I'm enough, world. Deal with it." That's not just Zen; it's *revolutionary*.

Stay Swaddled, Stay Supreme

So the next time life's too much—when your brain's a buffering icon and your soul's screaming "make it stop"—don't reach for a meditation app or a self-help book. Reach for the blanket. Wrap yourself tight, merge with the fluff, and let the chaos slide off you like water off a burrito's tortilla. You're not hiding—you're ascending, one cozy layer at a time. Stay there until further notice, or at least until you run out of snacks. Namaste, you swaddled, boundary-setting legend.

Zen Twenty-Six

CANCELING PLANS AS A FORM OF SELF-CARE

Obliterating Your Calendar Like a Zen Ninja with a Snack Stash

There's no thrill quite like opening your calendar, spotting a commitment glaring at you like a judgmental aunt at a family reunion, and then—*BAM*—wiping it out with one majestic swipe of your finger. It's not just canceling plans; it's a full-on spiritual emancipation, a middle finger to the tyranny of "showing up" when your soul's screaming for sweatpants and solitude. You had every intention of going—back when you RSVP'd "yes" in a haze of caffeine-fueled optimism, convinced you'd be a social butterfly with flawless small talk and pants that don't pinch. But now? Sober, spiritually drained, and staring at a pair of jeans that feel like a betrayal, you know the truth: those plans are unholy, the emotional labor is criminal, and your couch is your true soulmate.

Canceling plans isn't cowardice; it's a *radical act of soul preservation*, a masterclass in prioritizing your vibe over everyone else's expectations. You're not flaking; you're the Marie Kondo of social obligations, folding up invites that don't spark joy and yeeting them into the cosmic donation bin. This chapter is your sacred permission slip to become a cancellation ninja, slicing through commitments with the grace of a Zen monk and the pettiness of a cat who knocks over your water glass for fun. If it doesn't come with snacks or a vibe that screams, "I can wear slippers to this," cancel that sh*t with love and never look back.

The Cancellation Hierarchy: Your Guide to Ditching Plans Like a Pro

Not all cancellations are created equal. Like a fine wine or a perfectly stale bag of chips, your excuse needs to match the occasion. Here's your cancellation hierarchy, ranked from rookie to Zen master, to ensure you escape with your dignity (and Netflix queue) intact:

- **Level 1: The Classic Cop-Out** "Hey! Not feeling well." This is the beginner's go-to, emotionally accurate even if it's just your soul that's got a fever. Nobody's gonna argue with an emoji that screams, "I might be contagious." Use sparingly to avoid being labeled "that friend who's always sick." *Pro Tip*: Add a vague, "Might just need to rest up," to imply you're bravely soldiering through a crisis (aka binge-watching *Love Is Blind*).

- **Level 2: The Mysterious Conflict** "So sorry, a last-minute thing came up!" That "thing"? Your will to live, which just scheduled an emergency meeting with your couch. This excuse is versatile and unverifiable and leaves them wondering if you're saving orphans or just napping. Either way, you're free. *Pro Tip*: Throw in a, "Let's reschedule soon!" to sound like you mean it, knowing full well "soon" is a dimension you'll never visit.

- **Level 3: The Spiritual Flex** "My therapist said I shouldn't push myself right now." They didn't, but your inner therapist—aka the voice that says, "You deserve tacos, not trauma"—totally did. This is peak Zen, weaponizing self-care jargon to shut down any pushback. Who's gonna argue with your mental health? Not Karen, that's for sure. *Pro Tip:* Pair with a serene, "I'm just honoring my boundaries," and watch them back off like you're glowing with Dalai Lama-level wisdom.

- **Level 4: The Cosmic Veto** "The universe is telling me to sit this one out—bad Mercury retrograde vibes." This is for the advanced slacker who's ready to lean into full-blown woo-woo chaos. Nobody's fact-checking the stars, and you sound like a mystic who's too busy communing with the cosmos to deal with their wine-and-paint night. *Pro Tip:* Add, "My tarot cards were *not* vibing with this," for extra unhinged flair. Bonus points if you claim your cat flipped the Death card.

- **Level 5: The Blanket Burrito Blackout** Don't reply at all. Just vanish into your blanket fort like a hermit sage who's transcended earthly communication. This is the ultimate power move, reserved for when you're so deep in your slacker Zen that even typing "nope" feels like too much. They'll assume you're in a spiritual retreat (or dead, but either way, they'll leave you alone). *Pro Tip:* If they follow up, wait 48 hours, then text, "Sorry, I was in a silent meditation vortex." They'll be too confused to care.

The Art of the Flake: Crafting Your Cancellation with Zen Finesse

A masterful cancellation is like a perfectly executed heist—smooth, swift, and leaving no trace of guilt. Here's the formula to make your flake feel like a love letter rather than a slap:

1. **Start with Flattery**: "Your party sounds like it's gonna be the event of the century!" They're too busy blushing to notice you're about to bail.

2. **Drop the Excuse**: "But I'm slammed with a soul-level recalibration—think less 'busy' and more 'existential crisis chic.'" Keep it vague and spiritual; nobody's fact-checking your aura.

3. **Seal with Gratitude**: "I'm gutted to miss it; you're a legend for inviting me!" Now they're thanking *you* for staying home with your Doritos.

Example: "Your book club's gonna be lit, but my chakras are throwing a tantrum, and my therapist says I need to vibe solo. You're a star for asking—let's catch up when Mercury's less of a jerk!" Boom. You're free, and they're picturing you as a serene yogi instead of a couch goblin arguing with your Roomba.

The Cancellation Starter Pack: Gear for the Masterful Slacker

To excel at canceling plans, you need the right tools to maintain your Zen while dodging the world. Here's your kit:

- **A Cozy Couch Throne:** Your base of operations, complete with a stain named Greg and crumbs that spell "FREEDOM" in snack residue.

- **A Snack Stash**: Goldfish, stale pretzels, or that rogue Twix you found in your hoodie. Canceling burns calories, and you need fuel.

- **A Phone on Silent**: Bury it under a pile of laundry to avoid follow-up texts. If it rings, pretend it's the universe calling to confirm your flake.

- **A Blanket Burrito**: Wrap yourself in every throw you own until you're a cocoon of nope. Bonus if it smells like popcorn and existential dread.

- **A Vague Mantra**: Mutter, "I am honoring my energy," like it's a spell that banishes potlucks and small talk.

Handling the Flake Haters: Deflecting Guilt Like a Zen Boss

The world's crawling with social police who'll try to guilt-trip your cancellation game. Your friend texts, "You always bail!" Your mom calls, "Why can't you just show up?" Some LinkedIn bro in a $200 hoodie DMs you about a "networking brunch." Shut. It. Down. Channel your inner blanket burrito monk and respond with serene savagery:

- **To the Pouty Friend**: "I'm not bailing—I'm curating my energy for our next epic hang. Quality over quantity, babe."

- **To the Naggy Mom**: "I'm practicing radical self-care, Mom. It's like yoga but with more naps. Google it."

- **To the Networking Bro**: "My soul's booked for a solo retreat, Chad. Catch me when I'm less enlightened and more desperate."

For the relentless, whip out a glitter-pen sticky note that says "Boundaries" and slap it on their forehead like a Zen hex. Or just ghost them—Level 5 cancellation is a vibe all its own.

The Philosophy of Flaking: Why Canceling Is Peak Zen

Let's get deep: Zen is about living in alignment with your truth, and sometimes your truth is, "I'd rather wrestle a bear than go to your trivia night." Canceling plans isn't just self-care—it's *self-sovereignty*. It's saying, "My peace is non-negotiable, and your happy hour isn't worth my pants." The Buddha didn't RSVP to every village potluck; he chilled under a tree, vibing with his own soul. You're doing the same, just with better Wi-Fi and a snack stash.

Every canceled plan is a love letter to your nervous system, a vow to protect your energy from the chaos of forced fun. You're not just flaking—you're curating a life that sparks joy, one "nope" at a time. So keep canceling, you radiant, plan-ditching legend. Let your intuition be your guide, your couch be your temple, and your blanket burrito be your battle armor. You're not lazy—you're a cancellation ninja, a Zen rockstar, a poet of "not today."

And if anyone asks why you bailed, flash a wild grin and say, "I'm too busy honoring my soul to deal with your charcuterie board." Then saunter off, snack crumbs trailing like a Zen breadcrumb path. Namaste, you gloriously unavailable icon.

Zen Twenty-Seven
The Gentle Art of Not Giving a Sh*t

Liberating Your Soul from the Tyranny of Too Many F*cks

Let's be real: you're exhausted. You've been handing out sh*ts like they're free samples at Costco—worrying about your boss's cryptic email, your neighbor's judgy side-eye, or that time you accidentally liked your ex's post from 2017. You're mentally juggling so many pointless concerns it's like you're auditioning for the Anxiety Circus. Spoiler: you didn't sign up for this, and it's time to quit the gig.

Welcome to the gentle art of not giving a sh*t; *your ticket to emotional minimalism. This isn't about being a jerk or going full nihilist; it's about curating your emotional life like a Pinterest board, keeping only the sh*t* that sparks joy and yeeting the rest into the abyss. Think of it as soul decluttering: less stress rashes, more couch naps. So light a candle (or don't: effort's optional), and let's get you to a place so Zen you'll be smirking at chaos like a sloth on Valium.

The Sh*t-Giving Spectrum: Where Do You Fall?

First, let's figure out how deep you're in the sh*t-giving game. Are you a newbie sweating the small stuff or a pro who's already checked out of the drama hotel? Here's the rundown:

- **The Sh*t-Giving Novice**: You're up at 3 AM wondering if your "k thx" text sounded too harsh. You've apologized to your cat for stepping on its tail *and* to the mailman for existing. Your brain's a hamster wheel of "what ifs," and your heart rate's screaming "help."

- **The Sh*t-Giving Intermediate**: You've ditched caring about strangers' opinions on your TikTok dance, but you're still haunted by that time you said "you too" when the waiter told you to enjoy your meal. You're flirting with freedom but clutching a few sh*ts like security blankets.

- **The Sh*t-Giving Master**: You've got unopened texts from 2018 and zero regrets. You rock sweatpants to the grocery store and call it "vibes." When someone tries to guilt you, you just shrug and say, "Cool story, bro." You're basically Buddha with a Netflix subscription.

No matter where you land, we're leveling you up. Time to shed those extra sh*ts like they're skinny jeans in a world of leggings.

The Mantras of Minimalism: Your Toolkit for Not Caring

You need some slick one-liners to fend off the world's nonsense. Think of them as your verbal force field. Practice these until you can drop them with the chill of a penguin on ice:

- **"That sounds like a you problem."** Ideal for when someone tries to offload their mess—like your coworker griping about a project you didn't sign up for. Say it sweetly, and watch their brain glitch.

- **"Oh no... anyway."** The perfect exit ramp for drama, guilt trips, or your aunt's rant about her bunions. It's the verbal equivalent of hitting "skip" on life's ads.

- **"I simply cannot emotionally afford that today."** Use this to dodge obligations or lectures—like your friend begging you to join their MLM. Add "my vibe account's overdrawn" for flair.

- **"I honor your chaos by not absorbing it."** The ultimate Zen flex, perfect for when someone's meltdown is Oscar-worthy. Sip your coffee, drop this gem, and float away like a sage in slippers.

The Ritual of Release: How to Stop Giving a Sh*t in 4 Easy Steps

Not giving a sh*t is a skill, like napping or avoiding small talk. Here's your foolproof ritual to ditch the baggage and reclaim your chill:

1. **Identify the Sh*t**: Scribble down everything stressing you out—your boss's passive-aggressive "per my last email," your roommate's loud chewing, that awkward wave to a stranger. This is your sh*t hit list.

2. **Ask the Kondo Question**: For each one, ask, "Does this sh*t spark joy?" If it's not lighting up your soul like a puppy in pajamas, it's trash. Most sh*ts fail this test harder than a toddler fails naptime.

3. **Release with Flair**: Picture each sh*t as a tacky helium balloon—give it a shove and watch it drift off while whispering, "Not my problem, pal." Bonus points if you flick on a lamp for mood lighting.

4. **Celebrate Your Freedom**: Crack open a snack (Cheetos?). Yes, please, and sprawl out like the unshackled icon you are. You're not just lounging; you're thriving.

Sh*t-Free Scenarios: Living the Dream
Let's put this into practice with some real-world chaos:
- **The Overbearing Boss:** Your manager pings you at 6 PM with "urgent" busywork. Old you would panic. New you? "That's a tomorrow-you issue, Linda." Shut the laptop and grab a drink—your peace outranks their priorities.

- **The Nosy Neighbor:** They're glaring at your un-mowed lawn like it's a crime scene. Skip the excuses, hit 'em with, "I honor your chaos by not absorbing it," and saunter off. Maybe salute with a granola bar for effect.

- **The Social Media Trap:** You're scrolling past someone's "blessed" vacation pics and feel the envy creep in. Nope. Mutter, "Oh no... anyway," and keep scrolling. Your emotional Wi-Fi's too spotty for that noise.

- **The Family Guilt Trip:** Your cousin's mad you bailed on their BBQ. Instead of groveling, say, "I simply cannot emotionally afford that today," then text a peace-offering GIF. Their pout? Not your zoo.

Your Sh*t-Free Toolkit
To stay in the Zen zone, you need supplies. Here's your minimalist must-haves:
- **Couch Command Center:** Your HQ, complete with a questionable stain (sup, Gary) and a blanket nest of "nah."

- **Emergency Snacks:** Stash some chips or a rogue candy bar—sustenance for your sh*t-free soul.

- **Vibe Armor:** Pop on shades (real or mental) to block the haters. Smirk like you're untouchable.

- **Blanket Cocoon:** Burrito yourself in fleece and let the world's BS bounce off like rain on a tin roof.

- **Mantra Jams:** Queue up lo-fi beats or ocean waves—drown out the drama with chill vibes.

Sh*t-Pushers Beware: Deflection 101

Some folks will try to shove their sh*ts your way; it's their superpower. Here's how to deflect like a pro:

- **Coworker Whining About Work:** "Rough day, huh? My sh*t quota's full—try Steve, he loves a challenge."

- **Friend's Marathon Vent:** "Wow, that's a lot. I'm keeping my slate sh*t-free, so how about pizza instead?"

- **Relative's Nagging:** "Appreciate the input, but my emotional storage is maxed. See ya at the holidays."

For the relentless, just grin and say, "No sh*ts given," then vanish like a ghost with better plans. Silence is your secret weapon.

The Zen Payoff: Why This Rules

Not giving a sh*t isn't rude; it's revolutionary. Zen gurus have been preaching detachment for ages: drop what weighs you down. Hoarding sh*ts is like keeping expired coupons—useless and cluttered. By letting go, you're not heartless; you're *light*. You're choosing calm over chaos, and that's badass. Less sh*ts

= more space for snacks, sleep, and strutting through life like a legend.

Keep at it. Sip your tea (or soda—who cares), watch your stress fade, and own your sh*t-free glow. You're not aloof; you're a serenity rockstar. Chant it: "I honor your chaos by not absorbing it." Now go live your unbothered truth, you glorious slacker.

Zen Twenty-Eight

BE THE CLOUD. FLOAT. JUDGE NOTHING. RAIN OCCASIONALLY.

The Ultimate Guide to Cloud Vibes: Float Like You're Untouchable, Rain When You're Over It

Look to the sky. Not because it's got answers, because it's your new life coach, and it's serving *major* chill energy. Clouds don't hustle. They don't reply all to pointless emails. They don't spiral over whether their shape is "fluffy enough" or if they're blocking someone's precious sunbeams. They just *exist.* Floating, drifting, occasionally crying on a picnic like a petty ex who knows you forgot your umbrella. No one questions it. No one expects clouds to "optimize" or "lean in." They're just up there, vibing harder than a sloth on a spa day, and you, my friend, are about to steal their whole aesthetic.

Welcome to the cloud life, where your only job is to float above the nonsense, shade your peace when needed, and drop a thunderous "nope" when the world gets too clingy. You're not here to perform, hustle, or even *pretend* to care about Karen's potluck invite. You're here to exist ambiguously, judge nothing, and occasionally cause minor disruptions in someone's day—like a cloud casually ruining a beach trip. That's not chaos; that's *balance*.

That's wisdom. That's weather-based enlightenment, and you're about to be its poster child.

Why Clouds Are the Ultimate Zen Icons

Let's break it down: clouds are the OGs of not giving a sh*t. They don't have to-do lists, performance reviews, or existential crises about their purpose. They just *are*—and they're thriving. Here's what makes them the ultimate role models for your slacker-Zen journey:

- **They Don't Hustle**: Clouds move at their own pace, which is basically "whenever the wind feels like it." No rush, no deadlines, no "I'll sleep when I'm dead" energy. They're the embodiment of "slow and steady wins the nap race."

- **They Don't Care About Your Opinion**: Ever seen a cloud reshape itself because someone called it "too gloomy"? Nope. Clouds are out here serving whatever vibe they want—fluffy, ominous, or straight-up apocalyptic—and they don't ask for feedback. You're not here to be liked; you're here to *be*.

- **They Ghost Without Guilt**: One minute, a cloud's blocking the sun like a petty bouncer; the next, it's gone, leaving you squinting and confused. No explanation, no apology. That's the energy we're channeling—unbothered and unavailable.

- **They Rain When They're Over It**: Clouds don't hold back their feelings. When they've had enough, they let it pour, no permission needed. You, too, can drop a "nope" storm when your boundaries get crossed. It's not drama—it's *self-care*.

Clouds are the ultimate Zen icons because they've mastered the art of doing fckng nothing while still being essential. They're not out here trying to prove their worth; they're just floating, shading, and occasionally raining on parades. And guess what? The world keeps spinning. So why can't you?

The Cloud Practice Playbook: How to Float Through Life Like a Pro

Ready to channel your inner cloud and float above the chaos? Here's your step-by-step guide to living that effortless, judgment-free life:

1. **Float Above the Nonsense**: When drama strikes—like your coworker's meltdown over a missing stapler or your aunt's lecture on "getting your life together"—imagine yourself as a cloud, high above the fray. You're not ignoring the chaos; you're just too elevated to care. Pro tip: Squint like you're pondering the cosmos when you're really just thinking about pizza.

2. **Shade Your Peace When Needed**: Clouds don't let the sun bully them into disappearing. When life's demands start burning through your chill, throw some shade. Cancel plans, mute group chats, or just flop onto your couch like a defiant nimbus. Your peace is sacred—protect it like a VIP section at a cloud convention.

3. **Rain Occasionally (But Make It Count)**: Sometimes, you've gotta let it pour. When someone crosses your boundaries—like your roommate eating your last yogurt or your boss scheduling a 7 a.m. "quick sync"—drop a thunderous "nope." It's not a tantrum; it's a *boundary*

storm. Let it rain, then float on.

4. **Judge Nothing (Including Yourself)**: Clouds don't critique their own fluffiness, and neither should you. Spilled coffee on your shirt? Cool, it's avant-garde. Forgot to text back for three days? You're just practicing cloud-like detachment. Embrace the mess—it's all part of the float.

Cloud Practice in Action: Real-Life Scenarios

Let's see how to apply cloud vibes in the wild:

- **The Overbearing Boss**: They're piling on tasks like you're a pack mule. Instead of stressing, channel your inner cirrus and say, "I'm floating through my workload at my own pace—catch me when the wind's right." Then take a long lunch and stare at the sky for "inspiration."

- **The Nosy Neighbor**: They're grilling you about your weekend plans. Instead of oversharing, hit 'em with, "I'm just drifting—might rain, might not." Then float away, leaving them to wonder if you're a poet or just really into weather.

- **The Guilt-Tripping Friend**: They're mad you bailed on brunch. Instead of groveling, say, "I was too busy being a cloud—had to shade my peace." Then send a cloud emoji and call it closure.

- **The Social Media Spiral**: You're doomscrolling, feeling inadequate. Stop. Remember: clouds don't compare their fluff to other clouds. They just float. So log off, grab a snack, and let your vibe be as unfiltered as a storm cloud.

Your Cloud Practice Starter Pack

To live that cloud life, you need gear that screams "I'm untouchable but thriving." Here's your toolkit:

- **A Comfy Couch Throne**: Your float zone, complete with a mystery stain (sup, Greg) and a pillow fort of "don't even try me."

- **Snacks for the Soul**: Stash some chips or a rogue candy bar—fuel for your floating journey.

- **A Blanket Cocoon**: Wrap yourself in fleece and let the world's BS evaporate like morning dew.

- **A Vague Stare**: Look like you're contemplating existence when you're really just wondering if clouds get lonely.

- **A Weather App**: Optional, but it's fun to check the forecast and say, "Same," when it's "partly cloudy with a chance of meh."

Handling the Cloud Haters: Deflecting Drama Like a Zen Sky

Some folks will try to drag you back to earth—bosses, relatives, that one friend who's always "just checking in." Shut. It. Down. Channel your inner cumulonimbus and respond with serene savagery:

- **To the Micromanaging Boss**: "I'm floating through my tasks—catch me when I drift your way." Then take a "meditation break" (aka nap).

- **To the Overly Invested Relative**: "I'm just vibing like a cloud, Mom. It's a whole Zen thing—Google it."

- **To the Clingy Friend**: "I'm in my float era—might rain, might not. Let's sync when I'm less… atmospheric."

For the relentless, just smile and say, "I'm too busy being a cloud to deal with your thunderstorm." Then float away, leaving them to stew in their own drizzle.

The Philosophy of Float: Why This Is Peak Zen

Let's get deep: Zen is about detachment, about letting go of the need to control or be controlled. Clouds are the ultimate Zen masters—they don't cling to outcomes, they don't stress about their next move, and they definitely don't care if you forgot your umbrella. By embracing cloud vibes, you're not being lazy; you're being *liberated*. You're saying, "I'm here, I'm floating, and that's enough." It's the ultimate act of self-acceptance, a middle finger to the grind, and a love letter to your own damn peace.

Every time you float above the noise, you're telling the universe, "I'm good, thanks." You're not just existing—you're *thriving* in the art of doing f*ckng nothing, and that's the most enlightened flex there is. So keep floating, you radiant, cloud-like legend. Let your mood be partly cloudy with a 70% chance of not giving a damn. That's not just balance; that's *weather-based wisdom*. Namaste, you untouchable, occasionally rainy icon.

Zen Twenty-Nine
Sit. Breathe. Sip. Repeat.

The Sacred Ritual of Beverage-Based Enlightenment (No Incense Required)

Life is chaos. It's a dumpster fire wrapped in a group chat, set to the soundtrack of your neighbor's leaf blower and your inbox's passive-aggressive "just circling back" emails. You, however, are not here to spiral—you're here to sip your way to sanity like a goddamn deity of calm. Welcome to the sacred ritual of *Sit. Breathe. Sip. Repeat.*, a practice so simple it could make a Himalayan monk jealous and so effective it'll have your anxiety sobbing in the corner like a rejected contestant on *The Bachelor*. This isn't just a tea break; this is *soul hydration*, a masterclass in doing fckng nothing while looking like you've got the universe's cheat codes.

The ritual is as ancient as it is absurd: sit, breathe like you're not five seconds from a meltdown, sip something hot like you're the main character in a low-budget indie film, and repeat until the world stops screaming—or at least until your mug's empty. It's not procrastination; it's *strategic serenity*. So grab your favorite passive-aggressive mug, steep your vibes, and let's turn your living room into a temple of "I'm too Zen to deal with your drama."

Why This Ritual Is Your New Spiritual Flex

In a world where "self-care" usually means buying overpriced candles or pretending to like yoga, *Sit. Breathe. Sip. Repeat.* is the ultimate hack. It's mindfulness for people who'd rather nap than namaste, a way to ground yourself without leaving the couch or—god forbid—putting on pants. Here's why it works:

- **It's Stupidly Simple**: No apps, no gurus, no $200 retreats. Just you, a seat, some air, and a beverage. If you can fog a mirror and hold a cup, you're already halfway to enlightenment.

- **It's Customizable**: Tea, coffee, hot cocoa, or that weird herbal concoction your aunt swears cures existential dread—pick your potion. The only rule? It's gotta be hot, because cold drinks are for amateurs who don't understand the spiritual weight of steam.

- **It's Low-Stakes Zen**: You don't need to "clear your mind" or "find your center." Just sit, sip, and let the chaos melt like a forgotten ice cube. If your brain's still yammering about that email you ghosted, fine—sip louder.

This ritual isn't about escaping life; it's about *sipping through it* like a serene, slightly caffeinated cloud. You're not avoiding your problems—you're just too busy being a beverage-based deity to care.

The Ritual Breakdown: Your Step-by-Step Guide to Sipping Like a Sage

Let's dissect this four-step masterpiece of minimalism. Each part is crucial, like the ingredients in a spell—or the layers in a perfect nacho dip.

Step 1: Sit

Find a spot. Any spot. Couch, floor, that one chair with a mystery stain (sup, Greg)—doesn't matter. The key is to plant your ass like you're claiming territory in a game of musical chairs. Bonus points if you sit so still your cat thinks you've transcended and starts plotting to steal your snacks. Pro tip: If your sitting position looks like a rejected yoga pose, you're doing it right. Comfort over form—Zen doesn't care if your spine's aligned.

Step 2: Breathe

Breathe like you're not five seconds from a meltdown, which—let's be real—is a flex. Inhale like you're sniffing the secrets of the universe, exhale like you're blowing out the candles on your last fck to give. If your breath sounds like a sigh of relief or a groan of existential dread, perfect. You're not here to master pranayama; you're here to avoid screaming into a pillow. Pro tip: If your brain tries to spiral mid-breath, just wheeze louder; it's like white noise for your soul.

Step 3: Sip

Now, the sacred sip. Hold your mug like it's the Holy Grail (even if it says "World's Okayest Employee"). Take a slow, deliberate sip, like you're tasting the tears of your enemies or the elixir of eternal chill. Let the steam hit your face like a spa day for slackers. If your drink's got herbs you can't pronounce (Ashwagandha? Gesundheit), pretend you're a witch brewing calm. Pro tip: Spill a little for authenticity—enlightenment's messy.

Step 4: Repeat

Keep going until the universe stops being so damn loud—or until your mug's empty and you're too cozy to refill it. Each cycle is a mantra, a spell, a middle finger to the chaos. You're not just sipping; you're *recalibrating*. If you zone out and forget what step you're on, congrats—you've transcended. Pro tip: If someone interrupts, just sip louder and stare into the distance like you're mid-vision quest.

Bonus Points: Elevate Your Sip Game Like a Pro

For those ready to take their ritual to the next level, here are some advanced moves to make your sip session feel like a scene from a Wes Anderson film:

- **The Mug Flex**: Use a mug with a slogan like "I Can't People Today" or "Namaste in Bed." It's not just a cup; it's a billboard for your boundaries.

- **The Herbal Hoax**: Pick a drink with unpronounceable herbs (Turmeric? Ashwagandha? Gesundheit). You don't need to know what they do—just sip like you're curing your soul and watch people assume you're enlightened.

- **The Dramatic Stare**: Gaze out the window like you're in a low-budget indie film, pondering life's mysteries (or just wondering if your neighbor's dog is judging you). Bonus points if you sigh audibly and mutter, "The world's too much sometimes."

- **The Robe Ritual**: Wear a robe made of old tea towels or that one towel you stole from a spa. It's not a fashion statement—it's a *vibe*. Extra points if it's stained with yesterday's coffee.

- **The Sip Face**: Practice your "enlightened sip" in the mirror—think serene sage meets "I'm too cool for this." If you look slightly unhinged, you're nailing it.

Your Sip Ritual Starter Pack

To master this practice, you need gear that screams, "I'm calm but chaotic." Here's your toolkit:

- **A Mug with Attitude:** Bonus points if it's chipped or has a slogan that screams "I'm over it."

- **A Hot Beverage:** Tea, coffee, or hot water with a lemon wedge you found in the back of the fridge—anything steamy.

- **A Cozy Corner:** Couch, bed, or that one spot on the floor where the Wi-Fi's strong. Crumbs optional but encouraged.

- **A Blanket Cocoon:** Wrap yourself in fleece and let the world's noise bounce off like bad vibes.

- **A Vague Mantra:** Mutter, "I am the calm," like it's a spell that banishes emails and existential dread.

Handling the Sip Haters: Deflecting Chaos Like a Zen Barista

Some folks will try to crash your sip sesh—coworkers, relatives, that one friend who's always "just popping by." Shut. It. Down. Channel your inner beverage deity and respond with serene savagery:

- **To the Overzealous Coworker:** "I'm in my sip ritual—catch me when the steam clears." Then sip louder.

- **To the Nosy Relative:** "I'm communing with my inner calm, Aunt Karen. It's like yoga but with more caffeine."

- **To the Clingy Friend:** "I'm too busy being a deity of chill to deal with your drama. Let's sync when I'm less... hydrated."

For the relentless, just hold up your mug like a talisman and say, "This is my peace—respect it or get steamed." Then float away, leaving them to stew in their own chaos.

The Philosophy of Sip: Why This Is Peak Zen

Let's get deep: Zen is about presence, about finding stillness in the storm. And what's more present than sipping a hot drink while the world burns? You're not avoiding life; you're *anchoring* in it, one sip at a time. The steam? That's your worries evaporating. The warmth? That's your soul saying, "I'm good, thanks." It's not just a ritual; it's a *revolution*, a middle finger to the grind, and a love letter to your own damn peace.

Every sip is a reminder: you don't need to hustle, fix, or "optimize" your way to calm. You just need to sit, breathe, and let the universe sort itself out while you vibe with your mug. So keep sipping, you radiant, beverage-based legend. Let your mood be steamy with a 100% chance of serenity. That's not just balance; that's *beverage-based wisdom*. Namaste, you untouchable, occasionally caffeinated icon.

Zen Thirty

HOW TO PROCRASTINATE WITH PRESENCE

Procrastination gets a bad rap. People act like it's a flaw, a sign of laziness, or worse—a moral failing. But what if, stay with me here, what if it's actually... a form of *divine timing*? What if your soul is just waiting for the universe to align your chakras before you tackle that spreadsheet? What if the email you're avoiding hasn't *spiritually downloaded* yet, and the vacuuming is simply *marinating* in its own dust? Welcome to the Zen art of procrastination, where delay isn't a bug; it's a feature, a cosmic pause button, a sacred act of *doing nothing* with purpose.

This chapter rebrands procrastination as destiny, a holy excuse to stare at walls, fold laundry into abstract art, and research Icelandic sheep breeds while Steve from Accounting's email gathers digital dust. You're not avoiding life—you're preparing for it. Possibly for a snack. Possibly for nothing. And honestly, that's peak enlightenment.

The Sacred Art of Divine Delay

Let's set the record straight: procrastination isn't laziness. It's *intuitive scheduling*. It's your soul whispering, "Not yet, babe," while the universe rearranges the stars so your vibe matches the task. That project deadline? It's not due until your chakras say so. That inbox full of "urgent" requests? They can wait until your aura's had its coffee. And the laundry? It's not a chore—it's a *soft sculpture* waiting to be born.

Here's the truth: sometimes, the most enlightened thing you can do is *nothing*. Let the world spin without you for a hot second. The Buddha didn't achieve nirvana by answering emails on time—he sat under a tree and vibed. You're just following in his footsteps, minus the tree and plus a Netflix queue.

Procrastinate with Intention: A Masterclass in Mindful Delay

Procrastination isn't about zoning out—it's about zoning *in* to whatever your soul needs in the moment. It's mindful avoidance, a deliberate detour on the path to productivity. Here's how to do it like a Zen slacker:

- **Stare at a Wall with Deep Conviction**: Find a blank wall, lock eyes with it, and let your brain marinate in the void. This isn't wasting time—it's *wall meditation*. You're not avoiding your to-do list; you're communing with the drywall, letting its blankness inspire your next big idea (or at least your next nap).

- **Research Icelandic Sheep Breeds**: Instead of replying to Steve from Accounting's fifth follow-up email, dive into the fascinating world of Icelandic sheep. Did you know they have horns that look like they belong in a Viking helmet? Steve's budget report can wait—those sheep are living their best, unbothered lives, and you need to honor that.

- **Fold Laundry into Weird Shapes**: Turn your clean (or

questionably clean) clothes into *soft sculptures*. That lumpy pile of socks? It's not a mess; it's avant-garde art. Call it "Existential Cotton" and pretend you're a minimalist sculptor. The vacuuming can wait; your masterpiece can't.

- **Organize Your Snack Drawer**: Why tackle your inbox when you could alphabetize your chips? Doritos before Fritos, obviously. This isn't avoidance; it's *culinary curation*. Your future self will thank you when hunger strikes mid-existential crisis.

- **Watch Paint Dry (Literally or Figuratively)**: If you're feeling extra Zen, paint a small patch on your wall and watch it dry. It's not boring; it's *performance art*. If you're low on paint, just imagine it. Visualization is key to manifestation, right?

The Benefits of Procrastination: A Slacker's Manifesto

Procrastination isn't just a vibe; it's a *strategy*. Here's why it's secretly brilliant:

- **It's Brain Marination**: Your best ideas don't come when you're hustling—they come when you're halfway through a YouTube spiral about conspiracy theories or staring at your ceiling fan like it's a hypnotic oracle. Procrastination is just slow-cooking your genius. Let it simmer.

- **It's Energy Conservation**: Why burn out now when you can save your mojo for later? You're not avoiding work; you're *strategically pacing yourself*. Think of it as emotional budgeting: spend your energy wisely.

- **It's Guilt-Free Rebellion**: Society says, "do it now"; you say, "nah." That's not laziness; that's *subversion*. You're a rebel with a cause (the cause is snacks), flipping the bird to the cult of productivity.

- **It's Creative Fuel**: Ever notice how your brain spits out brilliant solutions right before a deadline? That's procrastination magic. It's like your mind's a pressure cooker, and the best ideas are the ones that pop out at 2 a.m. with a side of panic.

Handling the Procrastination Police: Deflecting Guilt Like a Zen Boss

The world's full of productivity cops—bosses, relatives, and that one friend who's always "crushing it" who'll try to shame your delay game. Here's how to shut them down with serene savagery:

- **To the Micromanaging Boss**: "I'm letting the project marinate—creativity can't be rushed." Then sip your coffee like you're a tortured artist who's too deep for deadlines.

- **To the Overachieving Friend**: "I'm practicing intentional delay; it's a Zen thing. Google it." Then float away, leaving them to stew in their own hustle.

- **To the Naggy Relative**: "I'm aligning my energy with the task. It's not ready for me yet." Then change the subject to Icelandic sheep; they'll be too confused to argue.

For the relentless, just smile and say, "I'm not avoiding; I'm preparing. The universe will tell me when it's time." Then yeet yourself into a nap. They can't guilt you if you're asleep.

The Procrastination Starter Pack: Gear for the Divine Delayer

To master procrastination with presence, you need tools that scream, "I'm busy doing nothing." Here's your kit:

- **A Couch with a Butt Groove**: Your procrastination throne, complete with a stain named Greg and crumbs that spell "YOLO."

- **A Snack Stash**: Goldfish, stale pretzels, or that rogue granola bar you found in your hoodie. Procrastination burns calories, and you need fuel.

- **A Blank Wall**: Your canvas for wall meditation. Bonus points if it's got a weird stain that looks like a Rorschach test.

- **A Playlist Called "Vibes Only"**: Fill it with lo-fi beats or whale sounds to drown out the noise of "you should be working."

- **A Mug of Something Hot**: Sip it slowly, like you're a sage pondering the mysteries of the universe (or just wondering if your cat's plotting against you).

The Philosophy of Procrastination: Why This Is Peak Zen

Let's get deep: Zen is about being present, about embracing the now without judgment. And what's more "now" than ignoring your to-do list to fold socks into avant-garde art? Procrastination isn't avoiding life; it's *living it*, one detour at a time. The Buddha didn't rush to enlightenment; he sat under a tree and let the universe come to him. You're doing the same, just with better Wi-Fi and a snack drawer.

Every time you procrastinate, you're telling the universe, "I trust you to sort this out while I vibe." You're not just delaying; you're *aligning*, letting divine timing work its magic. So keep procrastinating, you radiant, intentional delayer. Let your intuition be your guide, your couch be your temple, and your snack stash be your offering. You're not lazy; you're a Zen master, a divine delayer, a poet of "I'll do it later."

And if anyone asks why you haven't started, flash a wild grin and say, "I'm waiting for the universe to align my chakras. It's a whole vibe." Then saunter off, snack crumbs trailing like a Zen breadcrumb path. Namaste, you gloriously unhurried icon.

Zen Thirty-One

Spiritual Bloating and Other Mystical Conditions

Screw mountaintop monasteries and overpriced yoga retreats. The real path to enlightenment is paved with regretful nachos, a fart that could summon ancient deities, and a belly that's staging its own TED Talk. Welcome to the grand finale of doing f*ckng nothing, where you've expanded—not just spiritually or emotionally, but with the kind of gastrointestinal swagger that makes your stretchy pants pray for mercy. You lit incense, doodled about your third chakra, then swan-dived into a vat of garlic hummus like it was your life's calling. This chapter, the crowning jewel of *Outrageously Epic, Chill-Like-You-DGAF Paradise*, unveils the sacred, stinky truth: your gut is your guru. Sometimes, that ache isn't your soul crying—it's last night's queso plotting revenge. And that's not just fine; it's divine. Your higher self is throwing you a parade as you sprawl on the floor, clutching your bloated midriff, whimpering, "Why, tacos, why?" while your spirit whispers, "This is the f*ckng way." Let your gas be your gospel.

- **Farting Your Way to Nirvana**: Every toot is a cosmic haiku, proclaiming, "I am one with the multiverse... and yesterday's bean burrito!" Master the art of mindful flatulence: inhale tranquility, exhale a hurricane. Legend has it a monk once farted so hard in lotus pose he briefly orbited the monastery. Aim high. If you levitate, you're enlightened. If you just clear the room, you're still a DGAF deity. Warning: silent retreats will ban you, but that's their loss.

- **The Garlic Hummus Sutra**: Overeating isn't a mistake; it's a chickpeas-sponsored vision quest. When your gut roars like an angry dragon, don't fight it. Flop onto your couch, cradle a kombucha for Instagram vibes (it's pointless but chic), and chant, "This too shall pass." When it does—rattling the windows—bow. You've just composed a fart fugue Bach could only dream of. Your bloat is a masterpiece.

- **Burping the Mantra**: Forget "Ommm." Belch "BRAAAP" and rewrite the fabric of reality. A burp so seismic it cracks your amethyst geode, sends your cat vaulting over the couch, and makes your neighbor file a noise complaint isn't digestion; it's transcendence. Aim for operatic resonance. If you hit a note that shatters your kombucha bottle, you've unlocked the eighth chakra. Call it the Burp Chakra. It's real now.

- **The Lactose Lamentation**: That cheese board didn't betray you—it anointed you. As your gut stages a full-on opera, pen a haiku to mourn the dairy demon: *Brie, seductive fiend / Gut wails, throne awaits / I'm a bard, not a fool.* You're not in pain; you're crafting a saga. Your bathroom is now a Zen temple. Light a candle (carefully). Regret nothing, except maybe that second wedge of gouda.

- **Sacred Gas, Sacred Space:** Your living room is a cathedral, your stained sweatpants a robe fit for the Dalai Lama's chill cousin. Consecrate it with a fart so epic it parts your incense smoke like a biblical sea and makes your Roomba quit in protest. If your roommate chokes, smile beatifically and murmur, "I'm one with the void." If they flee, you've achieved ultimate Zen: a lease to yourself.

- **The Tummy Tantrum Koan:** When your belly rumbles like a death metal concert, don't meditate—bargain. Whisper, "Chill, gut, and I'll skip the kale smoothie." If it growls louder, you've met your true master. Bow (gently, don't jostle anything). Then eat another taco to assert dominance. Spoiler: you'll lose, but losing is Zen. Your gut is the real bodhisattva here.

- **The Bean Dip Bodhisattva:** You didn't "overdo" the seven-layer dip—you merged with it. Channel the Bean Dip Bodhisattva, who farted the entire Lotus Sutra at a potluck and ascended while everyone else gagged. Your bloat is your bodhi tree. Lounge beneath it (avoid sudden movements). Your farts are scripture. Preach.

- **The Queso Quest:** That late-night queso run wasn't a lapse—it was a pilgrimage. Each greasy spoonful was a step toward greasy nirvana. When your stomach stages a coup, don't panic. Visualize your bloat as a glowing orb of wisdom. If you fart and it sounds like a tuba solo, you've found the Holy Grail. If it just smells like regret, you're still a knight of nada.

- **The Bloat Meditation:** Sit cross-legged (or don't, who cares?). Close your eyes. Picture your fart as a lotus flower, blooming into the cosmos. Inhale peace. Exhale ... well, you know. If your gut gurgles mid-visualization, that's not failure—it's the universe giggling with you. Keep going. You're not meditating; you're rewriting enlightenment, one toot at a time.

Gut Enlightenment Cheat Sheet

- Farted in warrior pose without collapsing? +20 Zen points.

- Blamed the cat for your gas, and it worked? +15 chaos points.

- Penned a queso haiku while crying? You're Rumi's gassier cousin.

- Survived a hummus hangover without therapy? Ascended. Thrice.

- Levitated via fart? NASA wants you. So does Tibet.

- Convinced your boss your bloat was "kundalini awakening"? You're a DGAF demigod.

- Farted so loud your smart speaker apologized? You've hacked the matrix.

- Made your yoga teacher quit with one toot? You're the

chosen one.

And so, as you stagger from your couch-cathedral, belly still serenading the gods with its primal ballad, know this is just the opening act of your DGAF dynasty. Your farts are the battle cry of a soul too free to care, your bloat the badge of a warrior who's done nothing and done it fckng well. But the art of doing fckng nothing has wilder, weirder, *ballsier* mysteries to unleash—ones that'll make your gut's greatest hits sound like a timid warm-up. Stay gassy, stay pointless, and stock your pantry for the next revolution in epic, give-no-fcks enlightenment. Your colon, and the cosmos, demand it.

The path to comfort *is* the path to God.

Conclusion

Zen and the Art of Doing Fckng Nothing (and Doing It Well) has taken you on a rollercoaster of zen, zingers, and zero-effort mastery. From mastering the art of ignoring Jeff's "k?" to perfecting the No-Blink Stare, you've unlocked the secrets to a life where doing nothing isn't just an option—it's a freakin' art form. You've laughed in the face of chaos, waved crystals at needy coworkers, and turned your phone into a sacred shrine of unread notifications.

So, as you close this book (or toss it aside to nap—your call), remember: enlightenment isn't about climbing mountains or chanting mantras—it's about mastering the couch, the mute button, and the glorious art of giving zero fcks with a smirk. Go forth, you zen renegade, and live the dream where the only thing you're committed to is your next snack break. And if the universe sends a Monday morning your way, just yeet it into a lavender field and blame your spirit guide—because you, my friend, are officially too enlightened to care. Peace out, you magnificent slacker!

Appendix A
Frequently Unasked Questions (FUQs)

Nobody's asking these questions, but your overwhelmed soul needs answers. This sacred FAQ, make that FUQ, distills the wisdom of *Outrageously Epic, Chill-Like-You-DGAF Paradise* into snarky nuggets of nothingness. Use them to justify your naps, farts, and taco stains with Zen swagger.

Q: Do I need to meditate every day?

A: No. But sitting quietly and pretending to is highly encouraged.

Q: Can I be lazy and enlightened?

A: Not only can you—you're doing it right now. Congratulations.

Q: Is it normal to cry during naps?

A: Yes. It means you're hydrated, emotionally and spiritually.

Q: Should I start a podcast or just lie down?

A: Lie down. Always lie down.

Q: Is my fart trying to tell me something?

A: Yes. It's your gut's life coach, whispering, "Skip the meeting, eat a taco." Listen, or it'll bench you with bloat.

Q: Why does my bloat feel like destiny?

A: Because it is. Your gut's swelling is a cosmic orb, glowing with queso-fueled fate. Bow to it (gently).

Q: **Should I answer that email or nap?**

A: Nap. Emails are just other people's problems cosplaying as your priorities. Your couch is your guru.

Q: **Is my Roomba judging my taco crumbs?**

A: Definitely. But fart in its path and call it a "vibe cleanse." It'll quit or worship you.

Q: **Can I achieve nirvana in sweatpants?**

A: You're already there. Elastic waistbands are the Dalai Lama's secret handshake. Burn your jeans.

Q: **Why does my burp sound like a mantra?**

A: Because it is. Each "BRAAAP" is your chakras singing karaoke. Burp louder; scare your cat to satori.

Q: **Should I go to that party or eat tacos?**

A: Tacos. Parties are just loud emails. Grease is your gospel, and your couch is the guest list.

Q: **Is it okay to ghost my boss?**

A: It's not just okay—it's Zen. Reply "vibes" to their texts and ascend to inbox-free nirvana.

Q: **Why does my gut hate me after hummus?**

A: It doesn't. It's staging a chickpeas opera, with farts as the encore. Applaud with kombucha.

Q: **Can I nap instead of journaling?**

A: Journaling is just napping with a pen. Drool on your pillow; that's your soul's calligraphy.

Q: **Is my queso obsession spiritual?**

A: Duh. Each cheesy dip is a prayer, your gut's gurgle a hymn. Spill it? That's holy water.

Q: **Should I exercise or fart in yoga class?**

A: Fart. It's your aura's battle cry, clearing the room and your schedule. Downward dog, upward toot.

Q: Why do I feel Zen when I cancel plans?

A: Canceling is a mudra, flipping off obligation. Your couch high-fives you; that's enlightenment.

Q: Is my cat's glare part of my Zen path?

A: Yes. Its judgy eyes are your koan. Fart back and whisper, "We're one." It'll blink or bolt.

Q: Can I be productive and DGAF?

A: No. Productivity is a trap. DGAF is freedom. Mute your inbox and nap like a demigod.

Q: Should I clean my apartment or meditate?

A: Meditate on your crumbs. They're a mandala of sloth. Your Roomba's chaos is your mantra.

Q: Is my bloat a sign from the universe?

A: Totally. It's a nebula of nacho wisdom, farting constellations of nada. Wear stretchy pants; ascend.

Q: Why do I dream of tacos during meditation?

A: Your soul's a taqueria, serving greasy koans. Wake up, eat one, and call it lucid dreaming.

Q: Can I skip my Zoom call for a burrito?

A: Skip it. Burritos are sacraments; Zoom is purgatory. Fart mid-call and blame "tech issues."

Q: Is doing nothing really doing something?

A: Deep. But no. Nothing is nothing, and you're the fckng Picasso of it. Frame your naps.

Final Note: These FUQs aren't just answers; they're your bloat-soaked battle cry, your taco-stained ticket to pointless paradise. Let them fuel your slacker soul, and brace for the wilder, ballsier, burp-drunk Zen coming in your next DGAF epic. Stay lazy, stay gassy, stay legendary.

www.ingramcontent.com/pod-product-compliance
Lightning Source LLC
Chambersburg PA
CBHW050639160426
43194CB00010B/1739